Divination and Joy

Intuitive Tools for an Inspired Life

By Joan Rose Staffen

Cover Design by Susan Vaughn
"Big Bang" Acrylic Painting by Joan Rose Staffen
Chart Template Design by Alexa Kiehl
Illustrations by Scot Mackenzie

WriteStar Publishing
831 251-0866
1030 River Street, #311
Santa Cruz, Ca 95060

*The authors and publishers offer this information and methodology for the reader to consider,
but the authors and publishers do not assume any responsibility
for any actions the reader takes.*

ISBN-13:
978-1452839325

ISBN-10:
1452839328

Dedicated to
Adam and Danielle Staffen

To laugh often and much;
to win the respect of intelligent people
and the affection of children;
to earn the appreciation of honest critics
and endure the betrayal of false friends;
to appreciate beauty,
to find the best in others,
to leave the world a little better;
whether by a healthy child,
a garden patch or a redeemed social condition;
to know even one life has breathed
easier because you have lived.
This is the meaning of success.
—Ralph Waldo Emerson

Foreword

This feels like the thumb of God.
–Lara Sprinkles upon holding a pendulum

Each of us has direct access to the truth. *Divination and Joy* presents intuitive methods to access this knowledge. Like ancient maps and charts, the process leads us back to the center of our being, into the light of deeper wisdom.

The art of divining or dowsing with rods for water and minerals has been used for ten thousand years. The Tassili-n-Ajjer, 8,000 year old cave paintings in Libya, depict a man divining with a rod. In the Bible, Moses and his son struck the rod and found water in the desert. In Europe where divining with rods and pendulums is more widely accepted, both scientists and non-scientists have been exploring uses since the Middle Ages. More recently, in a UNESCO study sponsored in 1952, the French Nobel Prize Winner, Charles Richet concluded, "Dowsing is a fact we must accept."

Today, artists, teachers, homemakers, attorneys, real estate agents, health practitioners, and high tech managers have learned how to divine with pendulums. The coaching method taught in this book utilizes the pendulum and Intuitive Charts™ to help with decision-making. From the basic yes and no decisions to those more involved, such as how to create a satisfying home and love life or how to change negative beliefs to positive, this book helps us get back on track, clear life issues and re-discover fun and adventure in our lives.

According to Richard Webster, author of *Dowsing for Beginners*, the following scientists were successful dowsers:

- Leonardo da Vinci
- Sir Issac Newton
- Thomas A. Edison
- Dr. Albert Einstein

Table of Contents

Foreword   4

List of Charts   6

The Promise   7

1. Seek and Find Answers – *Simple Pendulum and*

   Intuitive Chart Instructions   9

2. Clarify Thoughts, Make Decisions, and Align with Spirit

   –Foundation Charts   15

3. Create the Ideal Home, Love, and Spiritual Life

   –Personal Charts   26

4. Delve Deeper– *Inner Mapping Exercises*   36

5. Give the Gift of an Intuitive Reading   40

Epilogue   47

Bibliography/Suggested Readings   48

Acknowledgements   50

Appendix: The Intuitive Charts   51

List of Charts

(In Appendix)

Foundation Charts – *Decision Making, Issues, and Thoughts*
Yes/No and Clearing (Chart 1)
Think and Act (Chart 2)
Time and Percent (Chart 3)
Primary Issues (Chart 4)
People (Chart 5)
Seek and Find Spirit (Chart 6)
Spiritual Guides (Chart 7)
Spiritual Tools (Chart 8)
Limited Thoughts (Chart 9)
Empowering Thoughts (Chart 10)
Blessings (Chart 11)

Personal Charts –*Love, Home & Life Issues*
Love and Romance (Chart 12)
Nurturing Relationships (Chart 13)
Parenting (Chart 14)
Feelings (Chart 15)
Home Arts & Responsibilities (Chart 16)
Home Problem Solving (Chart 17)
Gardening (Chart 18)
Personal Finances (Chart 19)
Healing Arts (Chart 20)
Life Transitions (Chart 21)
Letting Go & Death (Chart 22)
Your Own Chart (Chart 23)
Fun & Adventure (Chart 24)
Prosperity Problem Solving (Chart 25)

The Promise

After he rose from the dead, his twelve disciples and seven women continued to be his followers and went to Galilee, onto the mountain called "Divination and Joy." –The Sophia of Jesus Christ, The Nag Hammadi Library

At one time or another we all have been at the bitter crossroads. It can be the moment or the year when we lose a well paying job or a tired marriage and realize we have hit a stone wall. We have to move forward in our journey, but we don't necessarily know the way to do it.

How do we make the right choice at critical life junctures? If we've reached the ripe age of twenty we might notice we have made a few good, but some bad, or perhaps disasterous decisions, often unconsciously. At thirty we may realize we don't know what is best for ourselves or what possible harsh consequences could result from a decision. At forty we are just grateful when events go our way without understanding the why of it.

If we have learned anything it is that life is an intricate play and choices begin to look less black and white. Often we have to choose between two lesser evils. When money is tight, what gets paid? The rent or the overdue car and insurance payments? Do we forego the utility bill in order to buy Christmas presents hoping somehow the money will come?

We may decide to step out in life, and by doing so, see if the direction we are headed is good for us or not. Maybe this works for some, but many of us end up frustrated, angry, and burnt out. We may try replacing husbands or wives, jobs or homes, a faster computer or car. Some of us give up and become cynical or even worse, numb, sleep-walking through our days. Also in our fast-paced lives we are often given too many choices and are expected to make decisions at a rapid pace.

But what about the big questions that will set your life course, determine whether it is happy and fulfilled? Should you marry your girl friend? Buy a house? Move to a new town, state, or country? Change your job?

How do we make deicions? Most of us talk to our friends; process and hear other people's opinions; we research the internet; read books; and get expert opinions. But can others truly answer the major questions for us? When we make the decision to leave a spouse or a job, do we know for sure this is best for us?

We are bombarded by media,with good answers available for every situation. We have more knowledge and experts than ever before. But how do we sift through and understand the information to make wise decisions?

What if we marry the wrong person? Take a job we will learn to hate? Waste one year, five years, or even ten? If we have learned anything, it it that life is short. Too short.

Divination and Joy introduces a decision-making method to guide you on your life path and to help you access your own inner wisdom. The methods used are mysterious yet practical, and lead to a deeper understanding of your own self. They can help you:
- Find new love and nurture relationships;
- Create an ideal home life;
- Clear negative thoughts and choose empowering thoughts
- Parent your children;
- Solve prosperity problems.

The Promise
We promise that anyone can learn the methods presented here with practice and persistence. As your intuition is heightened, you will begin to know and trust what is best for your life. By seeking inner guidance and making good choices, you can overcome obstacles, find joy, and fulfill your life mission.

How I Began Using a Pendulum and Charts
Three and a half years ago, a business friend said, "You need to talk to this woman." That day she introduced me to Shakti Wilson, Spiritual Rsponse Therapist (SRT), minister, teacher and consultant. (SRT was created by Robert Detzler as a complete therapeutic and spiritual healing system.)

At the time, I was suffering from the loss of my husband, James Staffen, who had also been my business partner. I had been in traditional counseling, which had been a great help, but I was still not feeling whole. At our first session, Shakti used a pendulum and charts quite naturally and was able to access detailed information about my life.

Over the next few weeks, I had remarkable experiences, and began letting go of the past and processing my grief. In addition, I was able to begin a new life as a single mother and at the same time move forward fully in my business life.

Fascinated by what I saw, I learned how to dowse and use a pendulum, then signed up for her classes; a year and a half later, I became a SRT Consultant myself. As a result, I created the Intuitive Charts in *Divination and Joy* . Thank you Shakti for being my healer and teacher.

The stories found throughout *Divination and Joy* are true, with some names and details changed to respect and protect the privacy of individuals.

Chapter 1
Seek and Find Answers
Simple Pendulum and Intuitive Chart Instructions

Pendulum - a body so suspended from a fixed point as to move to and fro by the action of gravity and acquired momentum. –Random House Webster's College Dictionary

As an Intuitive Coach, I am continually surprised to find fellow pendulum diviners in all walks of life. Sally, a successful real estate agent, pulls one out of her purse to show me, saying "I use it daily." And Mark, a high tech manager, brings another from a pocket, a gift from his wise grandfather who wouldn't make a decision without one. I have met homemakers, doctors, students, scientists, artists, and intuitive counselors who use pendulums for decision-making. They have found it is an easy way of checking in with their own intuition.

The pendulum is a simple instrument that can help anyone discover quick answers and sometimes profound solutions to all types of challenges, from the mundane to the complex. Here you will learn to use the pendulum with charts to enhance your personal and professional life.

Pendulum use is a form of dowsing. You may be familiar with water dowsing, the art of searching for underground resources with a rod. Even today if you live in the country, you know that when you need to dig a well, you first call a water dowser. Dowsers walk your property holding a simple rod in front of them. They are able to tell not only where the water is located, but also approximately how deep the well will have to be dug. No one knows exactly how or why certain people are able to dowse and find water, but we do know that trained dowsers are highly successful in finding water, even when engineers can't.

In a similar way, you can be trained to use the pendulum utilizing the Intuitive Charts to find the right answers and solutions. Our desire is to teach and inspire you to use a profound, yet simple, decision-making system we call *Intuitive Tools*, which can help you access your creativity as well as your intuition, and thus, transform your life.

The energy, called ideomotor response, is what dowsers feel when they find water or minerals. This is what a pendulum user taps when the right answer is found to a question. The ideomotor response reveals subconscious and super-conscious messages from your higher self through subtle body movements. When you use the pendulum, you are not consciously moving the fingers, hand, or wrist, and it appears that the pendulum is moving on its own. This is the ideomotor response. With training you can learn to get yes and no answers, and to use the charts to answer specific questions.

In the business world today, the primary tool is the computer, a tool that makes it far easier for us to organize, communicate, and work. Our fingers type while our eyes focus on the screen, and our minds work in conjunction with the computer. In a similar fashion, while using the pendulum and charts, our hand holds the pendulum, our eyes focus on the charts, and our minds open to our intuitive senses.

The first time I picked up a pendulum it felt familiar to me, as though it was a tool I had forgotten that I knew how to use. I began trying it out on every challenge in my life, to see if it would work; and then found myself depending on it for making decisions about small matters, and then larger questions, as I trusted the answers I was given.

After developing the Chart System, I realized that using this process is a short cut, greatly reducing the time between understanding a problem and finding a wise solution to whatever dilemma presents itself.

The pendulum helps us to center. After working with the pendulum for a few minutes, people report a tingling energy moving in the hand and arm, and then seem to go into a quiet space, where they become receptive to the suggestions presented by the pendulum and charts.

Some will be able to use the pendulum easily, and for others, it will take longer to feel comfortable. We all have different experiences, but we guarantee that if you relax, and give yourself time, you will be able to use the pendulum. As my friend Shauna said, "It is so easy to use, it's surprising."

Purchasing a Pendulum

You can purchase a pendulum at a local metaphysical bookstore, jewelry, or crystal shop, or you can create your own. You can also use a pendant that you may already own. Try a variety of pendulums, because each is unique. From crystal to brass, from wood to glass, pendulums come in many shapes and forms. One French collector has over a thousand. Find what aesthetically appeals to you. When holding a pendulum, make sure it feels good in your hand. You'll probably want several different types!

How to Make a Pendulum

Making a pendulum can be fun. Find a pointed object that can be hung on a string. Make sure it appeals to you, such as a beautiful crystal, gem, or stone. Attach it to a four- to five-inch string, a silver or gold chain, or silk cord if you prefer. The weight of the pendulum should be in proportion to the weight of the chain or string, so that they are in balance with each other. For instance you would want to use a heavy chain with a larger pendant.

How to Center
Before using the pendulum take three to five minutes to center yourself. Relax and breathe. It may seem difficult at first, but focusing is the way to get correct answers.

- Close your eyes and take a few deep breaths.
- For the best guidance ask your higher self, your spiritual guide, or Spirit to come into your mind and heart.
- Lower your shoulders and ask your body to relax.
- Wiggle your toes and feel your feet on the ground.
- Breathe slowly and rhythmically.
- Feel the breath moving in and out.
- Inwardly say a short calming affirmative phrase; for instance, "I am at peace."
- Repeat the phrase saying it slowly for three to five minutes.
- If your mind wanders, and it probably will, bring it back to your affirmation.
- When you are ready, bring yourself back by wiggling your toes and opening your eyes.

How to Use the Pendulum
Anyone can learn how to use a pendulum. It is important to suspend the belief that you can't. Instead, simply imagine that you can learn to do this easily. Follow the simple directions below. (You can use this exercise with the "Yes/No" Chart located on page 16).

- If you haven't already done so, center yourself and relax. (See above.)
- Hold the top of the chain between your thumb and first finger.
- Let the pendulum hang perfectly still.
- Without physically moving your fingers, hand, or wrist, mentally ask the pendulum to move in a forward/backward movement or in the north/south direction. This movement is your *Yes* answer. (Occasionally, however, people have individual yes/no signals. If your pendulum indicates that your signal is different, create your own personal signal.)
- Mentally, tell the pendulum to stop moving.
- Practice mentally saying the word the word "yes" and moving your pendulum forward and backward. Do this a number of times until you are comfortable knowing that your pendulum is saying yes.

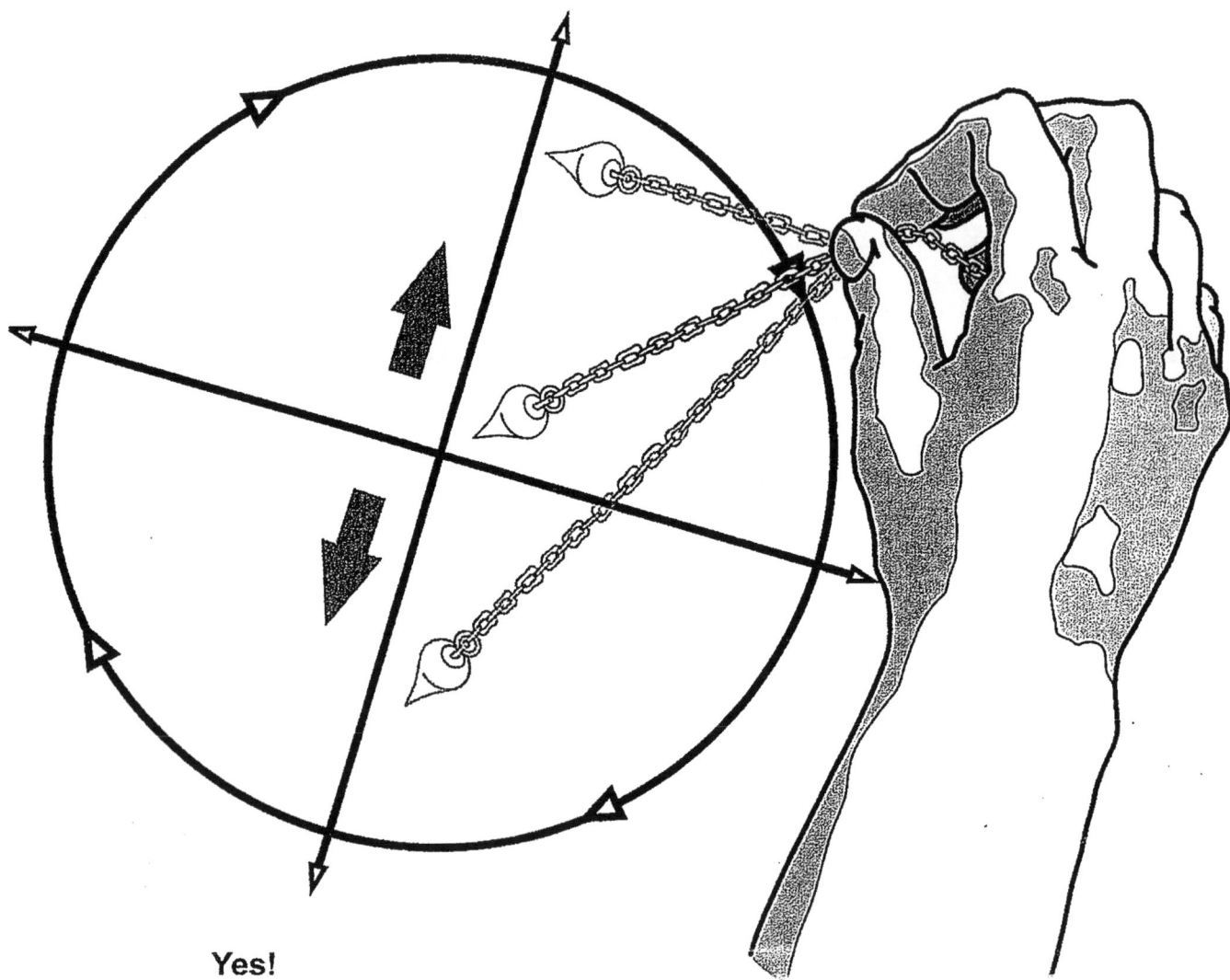

Yes!

- Mentally tell your pendulum to move side to side or in the east/west direction. This is your *No* answer.
- Next tell your pendulum to stop moving.
- Practice asking questions with yes or no answers. You can ask about a career choice or a relationship. For example: Am I in the right job? Should I consider other employment? Is there an opportunity for promotion in this position?

Continue to allow the pendulum to move without your hand or conscious mind influencing the decision. You may want to practice for a few days before exploring the charts. Or jump in and use the charts immediately. See how comfortable you are and move at your own pace.

How to Clear

Clearing with a pendulum is a one or two minute process to brighten, revitalize and strengthen our thinking. Leading busy lives we pick up negative, confused thoughts and messages that can cloud and muddle our minds. This can be either our own or other people's thoughts, ideas and expectations. We often move too fast and become scattered.

First learn the clearing "signal." Hold your pendulum between your thumb and first finger. Ask your pendulum to move in a clockwise position. Your pendulum will begin to move in a clockwise circular motion. As it does so, ask to clear your mind, thoughts and energy. If you feel comfortable take a few deep breaths, and close your eyes. The pendulum will move and circle. (See illustration on page x.) When it stops you know you are cleared. You will feel a bit sharper and more awake. (You can do the clearing with Chart 1.)

A woman I was teaching to clear said, " We could all use this five times a day! It's so easy and yet powerful."

Clear yourself prior to using the charts so that your answers are crystal clear.

If You Are Having Problems

If you can't get the pendulum to move, say the following sentence several times to clear your mind of skepticism:

I erase all doubting thoughts now.

Let your child mind come forth and imagine you can do it. If it still doesn't work, take a break and try later, when you are more open and relaxed. I have been in classes with fifty students, when within a half hour of practicing, everyone has been able to move the pendulum.

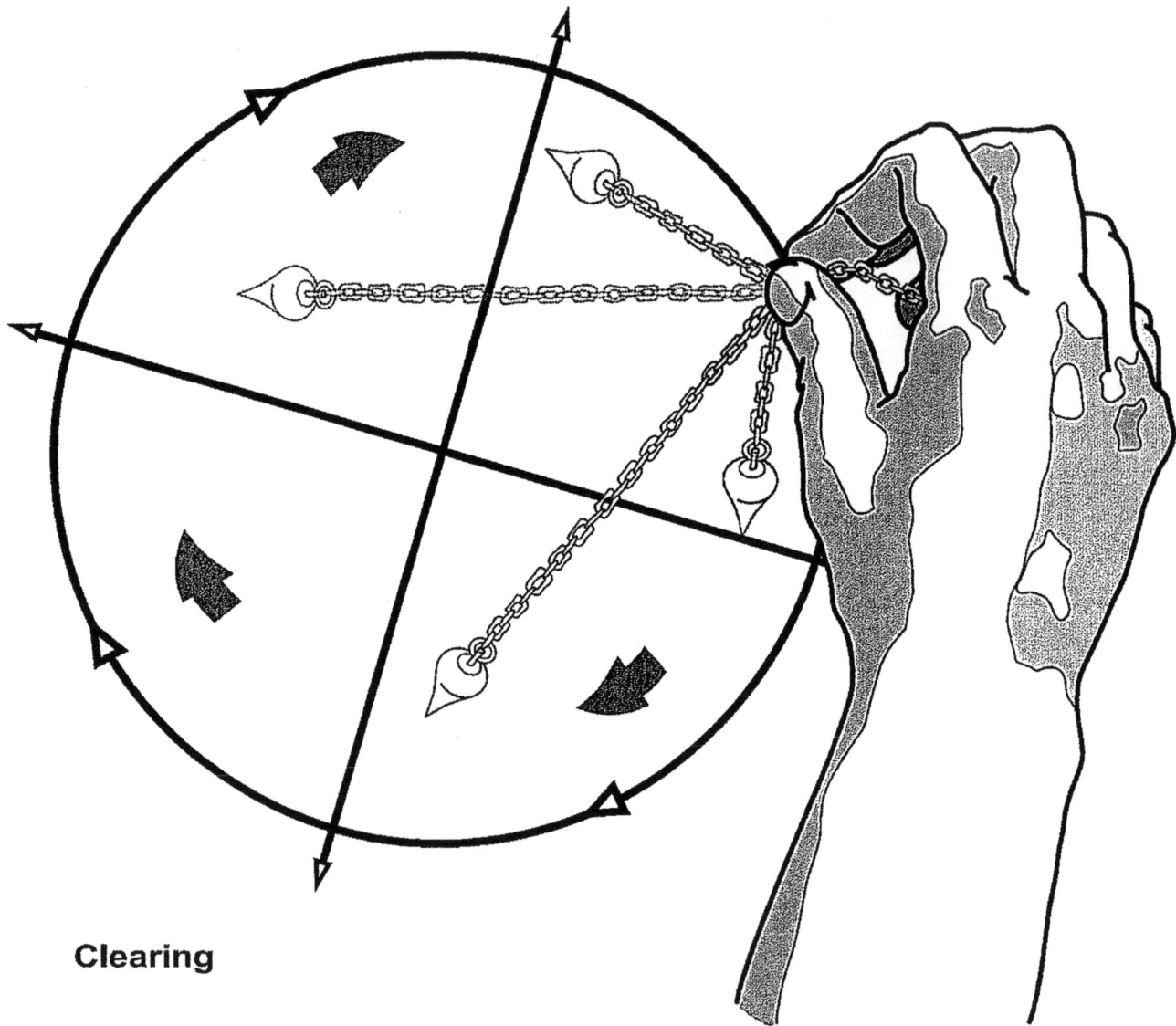

Clearing

Intuitive Charts

The next step is to learn to use the Intuitive Charts. These charts, developed to help in all aspects of your life, are divided into two areas and found in Chapter 2 and 3.

> • **Clarify Thoughts and Make Decisions**
> *The Foundation Charts* begin with the easy-to-use Yes/No Chart. Start to learn the basics here.
> • **Create the Ideal Home, Love, and Spiritual Life**
> *The Personal Charts* help you to create the best possible home life: assist you on finding new love, nurture your relationships, improve your parenting skills, and even resolve difficult transitions.

In these two chapters we introduce the charts with instructions following on how to use each one with sample questions to ask. We have included stories and practical advice relevant to our experience as Intuitive Coaches for Life and Business.

Take a few moments to turn to the end of the book and become familiar with the Intuitive Charts in the Appendix.

To Begin Divining with Intuitive Charts

- Center and Clear; see pages 13 and 14 for instructions.
- Start with the Yes/No Chart in the Appendix. Hold your pendulum over the center of the chart.
- As you learned, the *Yes* response is a forward and backward movement or north/south, and the *No* is a side to side movement or east/west. Ask questions that illicit a yes or no response.
- If you get more than one answer, ask for the pendulum to clarify and show you the most important answer.
- To check answers hold the pendulum directly over the word. The pendulum will circle in a clockwise manner as if the word is a magnet.
- Play and experiment. When you feel comfortable, begin experimenting with the charts.
- Look through the Intuitive Charts to see what interest you. Practice asking a question and receiving an answer. It's as easy as that.

Finding Answers

We turn to the charts because we have a question, an issue, or a challenge.

- **To Find a Quick Answer:** Go directly to the chart, ask your question and let the pendulum point to the right answer.
- **Intuitive Reading:** For a more complete reading, see Chapter 5.

Before beginning: center yourself, take a few deep breaths and ask using your pendulum: Am I working with my Higher Self? Are my answers 100% accurate?

If the answer is no, keep clearing until you are ready. If you are working on another person, always ask first: Do I have permission to work on this person? Is this for the highest good for this person? If the answers are no, say a prayer for them and place them in Spirit's hands.

If the Answers to Your Questions Don't Make Sense
- Even if the answers and charts to which you are guided don't seem to make sense in your reading, follow the pendulum's guidance anyway, and see where it leads.
- If the response seems totally off base, clear yourself, and ask Spirit for help.
- Take a break if you feel frustrated and come back to the process when you are more attuned.
- Occasionally, an answer will not make sense in the present but will in the future. Keep track of your answers.
- If you have further trouble, say a short affirmation and ask for one answer, or to be shown again.

Applaud Yourself
If you have trained your mind and pendulum to give you yes and no answers, and to clear, and you have begun using the pendulum with the Intuitive Charts, you are more than halfway home. Your effort is paying off. Have fun and be patient with yourself as you continue to trust your use of the pendulum and the answers you receive. Don't stop here, however. You are just getting into the juicy stuff.

Chapter 2
Clarify Thoughts, Make Decisions,
and Align with Spirit
Foundation Charts

Begin at the beginning and go on till you come to the end. Then stop.
–Lewis Carrol

In coaching clients over the years I have found that many of us need a five-degree adjustment in our lives. Have you ever felt that way? Like a plant that needs a bit more sunshine? By moving it into the light, it blossoms. By adding a few minutes of self-reflection to our morning routine, we continue to learn and grow.

The Foundation Charts can help you make a shift that, in the long run, will make your life bloom. You will feel more assured in the process, happier with your choices. From the Yes/No Chart to the Blessings Chart, this chapter will set your life on course.

Table of Charts

Table of Charts I and II are guides to all the other charts in this book. When looking for an answer, clarify the issue in your mind or on paper. Once the issue is clear to you, start your reading here.

Begin by holding your pendulum over the center oval and asking, "What chart is needed?" As you wait for an answer, keep your eye on the pendulum and let it guide you to the correct chart. Go to that chart; place the pendulum over the triangle or circle, and ask your question. After you are finished, return to the appropriate Table of Charts. Again ask, "What chart is needed?" Continue doing this until all of your questions are answered. When you return to the Table of Charts and the pendulum does not move, your reading is complete.

Remember: If more than one answer is given, ask, "Which chart should I go to first?"

Yes/No and Clearing Chart (Chart 1)

After the final no
there comes a yes
and on that yes
the future world depends.
No was the night.
Yes is this present sun.
　　　　　—Wallace Stevens, *The Well Dressed Man with a Beard*

Yes/No

Chart 1 is for questions with yes or no answers and for clearing negative energy. When learning, it is helpful to use the Yes/No Chart until you feel comfortable with the pendulum. When the pendulum moves forward and back, it means *Yes*, and when it moves side to side, it means *No*.

Clearing

Clearing our minds of clutter and negative energy is necessary when using the charts. Also, if you are feeling tired, stuck, or unbalanced, try clearing yourself. This thirty-second exercise can give you the lift you need morning, afternoon, or evening.

- Hold the pendulum at the center of the circle, and ask, "Please clear my mind, emotions, and spirit."
- Mentally tell the pendulum to move clockwise. This is your "clearing signal." (It is okay if it moves counter clockwise. You can choose this to be your clearing signal.)
- Let the pendulum circle; when it stops, you are cleared.

Practice using your pendulum to ask questions with yes or no responses about anything you might want to know. As soon as you feel comfortable, go to the other charts and practice as directed below.

Give Yourself Time To Make Important Decisions

For serious decisions always give yourself the right to make it the following day. Take the time to mull over a situation, especially one that is emotional or has great impact. Rarely does anything need to be decided on the spot. It is better to make the right choice, even if it takes additional time, than the wrong decision in a hurried manner.

Think, Plan, and Act (Chart 2)

What you do speaks so loudly that I cannot hear what you say. —Ralph Waldo Emerson

Chart 2 was created to give you options and answer questions you might be having. When you are stuck and don't know what to do, use this chart. Each of us has a particular strength. For some it will be planning, for others action. Some love planning so much, they fail to act. And others of us love to take action, and it would behoove us to do some planning. This chart will help correct those tendencies in us. When you are unsure of what to do, this chart will make clear what the best course of action is.

Suggested Questions to Ask
- What should I do?
- Is there anything else I need to consider?

The Answer Will Come
What if, after going through this process, you still don't know what to do? What you might want to try is clearly outlining the challenge on paper or the computer, and then asking Spirit for the correct action. Attempt to stop obsessing about the problem by distracting yourself with another project. Then just let go. You will usually be given an answer within 24 hours. You can always verify the information by using the charts.

As Albert Einstein said, "The significant problems we face cannot be solved at the same level of thinking we were at when we created them." Be patient, and let the answer come.

Time and Percent (Chart 3)
Nothing is ours except time. –Seneca, *Epistles*

Time
We always want to know when an event is going to take place; certainly decisions could be made more easily if we did. But often we cannot predict when someone is going to take an action in a given situation. You can use this chart to find out the general timing of an event. Know this can change, because people change their minds!

Question to Ask
What is the general time frame of this event, project, or situation?

Percent
Not only do we want to know when an event is going to take place; we'd like to know the likelihood of it taking place. Chart 3 will answer questions such as how likely it is that a boy friend will call to make a date, how well you will like a job, or the likelihood you will be moving soon.

Suggested Questions to Ask
- What is the possibility this event, project, or situation will move ahead?
- Does the event, project, or situation need to be cleared? If so, use the simple clearing method on page 18.
- Ask again, what is the likelihood of this event, project, or situation moving ahead? Sometimes, because you have performed a clearing the percentage of success will increase dramatically.

Because we are constantly creating our own reality and others are creating theirs, predicting time and actions can be difficult. The universe is fluid, not fixed. Know that this is a general answer, rather than a final answer.

Asking Spirit for Divine Order in Your Day
What you will notice is that if you ask Spirit for help in arranging your day and life, then you can accomplish all that needs to be done. Write a list of everything you want to do and ask for divine order in the day.

Often the people you need to talk to will then call. Books will be placed in front of you when needed to answer questions. When you're late for an appointment, say to Spirit, "Please help get me there on time." This is no small feat for busy at-home moms or working folks. By asking Spirit for assistance, the most important tasks are accomplished in loving, harmonious ways.

Primary Issues (Chart 4)
Where is there dignity unless there is honesty. –Marcus Tullius Cicero

Use this chart to inventory the key challenges in your life. The more honest we are with ourselves, the more quickly we can move through an issue. Most of our pain derives from resistance to the idea that we have to change. Awareness and acceptance of a problem is half the battle. Combining awareness with openness and willingness to find new solutions is the key to overcoming the hills and valleys we all have to traverse.

Now take a deep breath, get honest, and be willing to see your own truth.

Suggested Questions to Ask
- What do I need to look at?
- What do I need to be more honest about?
- What is the primary issue?
- What is the secondary issue?

By checking in and aligning with spirit, you will find that taking care of yourself and your loved ones begins to come naturally. The following three Foundation Charts help you find this spiritual direction to create the life you have always wanted.

People (Chart 5)
He who knows others is wise. He who knows himself is enlightened. –Lao Tzu, *Tao Te Ching*

Relationships can be the most challenging and rewarding aspect of life. We sometimes think: "If only *they* would leave us alone! Quit *their* job, or just leave." Do you ever feel that way? We may find ourselves with people we wouldn't necessarily have chosen to spend eight hours a day with; in such cases, life can feel pretty crazy.

When a difficult person (or situation) reminds us of someone else with whom we have unresolved, or painful, feelings, we may react with too much emotion. And, if raw emotions are buried, they often resurface inappropriately. Use Chart 5 to help research and discover who or what you are truly having an issue with and use the following exercise to find resolution.

Research and Resolve People Issues
To examine and solve a problem, go to the following charts and ask,
- People Chart: Who is the problem with? Is the problem with anyone else?
- Issue Chart: What is the issue?
- Limited Thoughts Chart: What is the thought I am holding?
- Empowering Chart: What thought will heal my mind?
- Table of Charts: What else do I need?

One day, Susan's girl friend, Roberta, stopped calling and talking to her. Susan e-mailed and asked what the problem was, but Roberta never answered. Susan used the method above and received the answers: *sister, abandonment* and *trust*. She realized her girl friend was like a sister, and she felt abandoned.

Susan thought back and remembered fifteen years before, the time in high school her sister had dumped her for the popular kids, and left her to walk home alone. Using the pendulum, Susan cleared the old memory, and replaced it with *trust*. By recognizing and understanding her own emotional pain, Susan was able to let go and move on. Now, while she still misses Roberta, Susan believes that new friends will come into her life.

A second method is to identify what it is in that other person that you dislike so much. Perhaps it is a part of yourself you don't like, a shadow aspect. For further resolution, use the mapping exercise, "The Shadow Self," in Chapter 4 to resolve the problem.

If you can't let go of the issue, a third approach is to create a positive affirmation or prayer that you say daily. Watch how the individual seems to change, and how your attitude towards him or her can change as well. If you cannot do this, pray for the willingness to do it.

Sharlene, was a single mom who had been harassed by her ex-husband for years; a long, sad story. She used this technique by making it a part of her daily prayers. Finally there was peace between the two of them, and they were able to share the parental responsibilities in a loving way. Sometimes we have to grit our teeth to do it, but the effort pays off. You will find freedom from resentment and anger.

Suggested Questions to Ask
- Who is the primary person involved in this situation?
- Is anyone else involved? If so, who?
- Does this person remind me of anyone in my family? (Mom, dad, or sister/brother?)

Seek and Find Spirit (Chart 6)
We could not seek God unless he were seeking us. We may begin to seek him in desolation, feeling nothing but His absence. But the mere fact that we seek Him proves that we have already found Him. –Thomas Merton, No Man is an Island

Whether it is because of the birth of a child or a personal tragedy, many of us begin a spiritual quest at some point in our lives. This can happen at age eight in a field of wild flowers, or at eighty on a deathbed. We might ask: Who am I? What is life all about? Does God exist?

The Seek and Find Spirit Chart contains a seven-step method based on the Twelve Steps of Alcoholics Anonymous, a popular program that has helped millions find new direction. Chart 6 will help you develop a relationship with the Higher Power of your own choosing. Ask what you need to work on or just start on step one below. This is the short version of climbing to the top of the mountain. Let it be a beginning.

- Awaken: Through pain or joy, powerlessness and/or rebirth, as you awaken you will begin to notice the love and beauty around you, in yourself and others. As if living in a new dimension, the life connections and intricate design of nature will become more evident. Ponder these questions: Who is responsible? Is it possible that a creator exists, and that there is a divine plan?
- Ask for Help: If you doubt, ask for spiritual help with a problem, large or small. Wait to see the answer appear in a synchronistic way. This is your Higher Power saying hello. (You get to name your Higher Power – Spirit, God, Goddess or any other name you choose.)
- Surrender: Let go of your ego (EGO = Easing God Out). This is easy to say, much harder to do. Ask that Spirit take charge of your ego, that selfish, demanding, critical mind that gets in the way, whose motto is "me, me, me." If you find yourself in the center of every drama, say, "I surrender my life and ego to the care of Spirit." Let go and let Spirit. P. S. Not to worry, you are giving up your little self to find your true Self.

- Inventory the Past: Write down with whom you are resentful, what happened, and how it affected you. Include yourself on the list. Then share this with someone you trust. Make a second list of every good quality you possess.
- Ask Forgiveness from Spirit and Others: First ask Spirit for forgiveness of the past. Then make amends to your family, friends, and others. Reread your list of the good qualities you possess while doing this process.
- Practice Daily: Spend five minutes in the morning with Spirit. You can sit in silence, read inspirational books, or meditate on the good in your life. Some people do this before they get out of bed and others over a cup of coffee or tea. Spirit just wants you to check in. She can help you throughout the day. Then give thanks at night before sleeping.
- Be of Love and Service: Ask your Higher Power how you can be of love and service. You will be guided to help others, and in doing so, will be less focused on yourself. This will help you get out of your ego mind.

Jeff, a man in his forties, lost his wife to suicide. Three years after her death he was still deeply angry, but unaware of it; he thought he had handled his feelings. Jeff wanted to start dating, but every time he talked to a pretty woman, he would find himself curiously numb. I did a reading for him on the phone, and was directed to the Seek and Find Spirit Chart, which gave me the answer, *Ask for Help.*

When I told him, he said, "I tried counseling, and the counselor was more interested in his own problems. It was a waste of money." I checked the Practical and Spiritual Tools Chart (Chart 8), and it suggested *Books.* He told me he'd be willing to read about others who had gone through similar situations, and start on the road to healing.

Suggested Questions to Ask
- Where should I begin in the process?
- What do I need today?
- What else would be helpful?

Spiritual Guides (Chart 7)
There is guidance for each of us, and by slowly listening we shall hear the right word. Place yourself in the middle of the stream of power and wisdom which flows into your life. Then without effort, you are impelled to truth and to perfect contentment. –Ralph Waldo Emerson

Chart 7 is for those of us who want to know what spiritual help is available in any given situation, reminding us that we have much more support than we ever imagined. You can quickly find out what spiritual guides are with you and can spend a few moments with them. If so inclined, ask for what you or another need or want. You will feel re-energized after a short meditation. Often new ideas and help will come when you least expect it.

Suggested Questions to Ask
- Who is helping me in this situation?
- Whose help do I need?
- Who can I call on when I need help?
- Who can I ask to help my friend, sister, brother, etc.?

Spiritual Tools (Chart 8)
Come to the edge, he said. They said, We are afraid, Come to the edge, he said. They came. He pushed them, and they flew... —Guillaume Applinaire

It takes tremendous energy and vitality to be a parent, a teacher, a construction worker, or an office worker. After all the demands of home and office, it is the provider who needs to take a break and revitalize. Are you giving yourself time to renew? This chart offers remedies to help in our daily lives.

A walk in the park during the lunch hour of a busy day can change your perspective. Ironically, during these mini-breaks, a solution to your problem may appear, or you may have a breakthrough on a major dilemma. So whether you're the parent of three young children, or a boss of a small, but busy company, remember to give yourself a daily break.

Suggested Questions to Ask
- What do I need for myself today?
- What would be most beneficial over the long term?

Limited Thoughts (Chart 9)
Fear is the little darkroom where negatives are developed. —Michael Pritchard

Often what holds us back is a limited thought. The mental, emotional and psychic chains we create prevent us from moving forward when that is what we most want and so desperately need. Have no fear; there is a simple solution.

Use Chart 9 to discover the limited idea. It is sometimes surprising to find that a fear from childhood has been lodged in our minds as truth. "We need mental floss," as Beyondanda, a humorous metaphysical teacher, likes to say. By identifying and clearing a thought, idea, or fear, we can set ourselves free.

Changing Limited Thoughts

Our thoughts have an incredible impact on our lives influencing us both positively and negatively. If you set up a goal or intention, it is important to identify what thoughts are behind it. Often we are being run—unconsciously--by old, unproductive thoughts we picked up as children; thoughts so ingrained we don't realize that we are repeatedly giving ourselves negative messages, such as: "I am always going to be poor."

For example, what if your goal is to save money for a new car, and your subconscious is imbedded in *lack*? What will show up for you? Nothing. What if you want a new job, and you think, " I am not good enough." What will show up? Nothing. We cannot create from a place of limited thoughts.

Whether you are fifteen, twenty-five or fifty, it is vital to have a positive attitude, and the ability to clear any negative thoughts for yourself. You are what you think.

Suggested Questions to Ask
- What thought or feeling holds me back?
- What is hard for me to look at?
- Is there something I am not being honest about?
- What thought do I need to let go of?
- Is there anything else keeping me from my good?

Grandma Moses (1860-1961)
Grandma Moses began painting rural scenes when she was in her seventies, and continued until her 100th year. She became the icon for American folk art. "I made the best out of what life had to offer. Life is what we make it, always has been, always will be."

What are you putting off doing because you think that you are too old?

Empowering Thoughts (Chart 10)

The basis of optimism is sheer terror. —Oscar Wilde

It cannot be emphasized enough how powerful words and thoughts can work for good in our minds and hearts. The words on Chart 10 are offered to help you change your thoughts and direct them in positive, new directions.

Suggested Questions to Ask

- What words do I need to empower myself today?
- What words will help heal this situation?
- What words will help _____ (fill in the blank)?

How to Replace a Negative with a Positive Thought

Check Chart 9, the Limited Thoughts Chart, and ask:

- What negative thought am I holding on to?
- What is blocking me?
- What thought needs to be cleared?

Use your pendulum, and ask to clear the negative thought. You will see your pendulum moving in a clockwise motion. Next go to Chart 10, Empowering Thoughts, and have your pendulum choose one or two words. Take a moment, close your eyes, and breathe in the positive thought. Then write yourself a strong affirmation, and repeat it throughout the next week.

I told a friend, Jay, whose body was aching from construction work, that I would do a clearing on him the next time I was using the Intuitive Charts. Two hours later, I sat down and did a short reading for him. I was guided to the Limited Thoughts Chart and asked, "What negative thought is Jay holding onto?" and was given the answer "Anger." At the Empowering Thoughts Chart, I asked, "What thought does he need?" and I was given the answer, "Willingness." I cleared the negative idea using my pendulum and in a 30-second affirmation asked that he be given the gift of willingness. Coincidentally, he called five minutes later to tell me how great his body felt and how all his aches and pains were gone. I laughingly said to him, "What a coincidence," and told him about the reading.

Powerful Words Meditation

The words and thoughts we repeat to ourselves help to support our greatness. Let's begin by using positive, energizing words. Take a few moments to settle in your chair and focus on your breath.

- Ask yourself what word or idea you would like to focus on today (powerful, confident, smart, authentic, energetic, etc.).
- Imagine in your mind a still, calm lake into which to drop these words and thoughts.

- Make a simple statement to repeat, starting with, "I am." For example: "I am totally at peace when I am working."
- Inhale, and silently repeat to yourself, "I am."
- Exhale, and silently repeat to yourself, "totally at peace when I am working."
- See the words dropping into the deep lake of your being, becoming a part of yourself.
- Repeat this cycle for five to ten minutes.

Blessings (Chart 11)

"I would lie in bed at night and say the alphabet, counting all the things I had to be grateful for, starting with the letter A...This made a great change in my life. –From *As We Understood* (An Alanon Book)

What would you like to be blessed with today? Or would you like to know what your Higher Power would like to give you today? Use Chart 11 to find out. You merely need to ask. It is fun waiting to see what occurs in the next twenty-four hours.

Suggested Questions to Ask
- What would Spirit like to bring me today?
- What would Spirit like to bring me this year?
- What blessing would improve my life?

Chapter 3
Create the Ideal Love and Home Life
Personal Charts
Everyone has a life. –Vickie Assunto, MFT

Sometimes we work so hard, we forget, we have a personal life. This set of charts reminds us that in order to get the most out of our lives we need to put time and energy into them. Do you want to fire up your love life or find solutions for parenting problems? Improve your home environment or plant a garden? The personal charts challenge you to look more closely at your life, find your own answers, and move to the next level.

Love and Romance (Chart 12)
Love is friendship set on fire.–Jeremy Taylor

Are you tired of waiting for the great love? Start here to find out how to get back in the game. Whether you need a friend, lover, or marriage partner, this chart will help you attract new love. Chart 12 is for single people with romantic hearts who know a soul mate is coming although he or she is a little late. Remember to let go and forgive the past, open your heart and mind, and to use discretion. This chart will help prepare and then move you through the early stages of romance. May you find the right person to hold you!

Or if you've been with the same person for some time, Chart 12 will help you rekindle the flame. Give the chart a chance to speak to your heart, so you can offer yourself fresh new ways to put the romance back into your marriage.

Suggested Questions to Ask
*   What do I need to let go in the past?
*   Who do I need to forgive?
*   How can I prepare for my next relationship?
*   What qualities do I want in my partner?
*   How do I attract a new partner?

Nurturing Relationships (Chart 13)
Sometime it is necessary to re-teach a thing its lovliness...until it flowers from within... –Galway Kinnel

What can enrich our lives, save our relationships? Become conscious of the importance of creating time for others, and giving attention to our loved ones. In the end we never regret that we spent too little time at work; rather we wish we had spoken more intimately to friends and family, cuddled with

we wish we had spoken more intimately to friends and family, cuddled with our kids at night, and danced with our true love to a slow, sweet song. Surprise and delight those you love.

Tanya, a young mother with a baby and a toddler, wanted to know what she could do to improve her relationship with her husband, Jonathan. She asked the questions below and received clear answers. Two were especially helpful to her. They were, *See the Best in Each Other* and *Take Time Together*. During the session she realized they hadn't had a date since the baby was born. That Saturday night Tanya put on a slinky dress, and Jonathan dressed in his favorite sport jacket. After their seafood dinner on the wharf, they took a long walk on the beach. Though they were only gone three hours, Tanya reported she felt like she got her husband back. Now they make a conscious effort to have a date at least once a week.

Suggested Questions to Ask
- What is working?
- What is lacking?
- What do I need to ask for?
- What can I give?
- What will help us?

Parenting (Chart 14)
I regard (parenting) as the hardest, most complicated, anxiety-ridden, sweat-and-blood-producing job in the world. Succeeding requires the ultimate in patience, common sense, commitment, humor, tact, love, wisdom, awareness, and knowledge. At the same time, it holds the possibility for the most rewarding, joyous experience of a lifetime, namely, that of being successful guides to a new and unique human being. –Virginia Satir (20th century), U.S. family therapist and author.

Everyone has had a parent and certainly has opinions on how to raise children, but in the moment to moment trenches of parenting, we sometimes become the tantrumming two year old while attempting to drag our screaming child from the grocery store. But as we grow in our own parenting skills, we will notice that there is an mixture of moments that range from incredible frustration to outrageous joy. Children at all stages from birth to adulthood have lessons to teach us, including love, patience and understanding.

As we parent our children, to a certain extent we relive our own childhood. We can heal from our own traumas by being the parent we ourselves wanted.

27

Suggested Questions to Ask
- What is working?
- What do I need right now?
- What does my child need?
- What is best for the family?
- What am I failing to do?
- What am I doing well?

Feelings (Chart 15)
Anger can lead to action; love to a gentler life. ¬Joan Staffen

Chart 15 lists forty-two emotions, from love to betrayal.

Sometimes we don't know what's going on inside ourselves. Feelings and emotions are part of our human make up, as real as organs and bones; however, they are often elusive, perhaps partly imagined, especially when we react to an old sadness or wound.

Just knowing what we are feeling can offer relief. Then we can process by talking with a friend or partner, and use the Intuitive Charts to find solutions. When there are strong emotions, pay attention. Your feeling-self is giving you a message: this is important. Dig deeper, and find your truth.

Intuition and emotions have always been linked. The more we are in touch with our Inner Self and its messages, the more we can steer through a myriad of challenges.

And lastly, *feelings are not facts.* If you are overreacting, pull back, take time apart, and examine--preferably with the help of others--what the unburied wound might be. Though it doesn't always feel possible, you can help yourself out of the dark places your mind may have traveled to. When you take action by following the suggestions of the charts, you will be rewarded, able to face yourself; and beneath the pain, you will find self-awareness and a new freedom.

Use Chart 15 to help you sort mixed feelings about people and events. Then go back to the Table of Charts I and ask, "What will help lift me?" Clear yourself, do the work suggested and if possible get support from a friend.

Years ago, Patricia had been left at the altar by her fiancée. A few weeks before the wedding, he picked a fight with her and left in a rage, saying it was over. Though they did eventually talk, she was never able to entirely let go and heal. We asked what she was feeling; it was *Sadness.* Then led to the Spiritual Tools Chart (Chart 8), she was given the answer, *Prayer.* Patricia and I, right then and there, asked that she now be released. Six weeks later, Patricia met a new man. They are taking it slow, and she is having the time of her life.

Suggested Questions to Ask:
- What am I feeling? (Feelings Chart)
- What feeling(s) will lift me? (Feelings Chart)
- What else do I need? (Table of Charts)
- How can I release myself from this? (Table of Charts)

Home Arts (Chart 16)

The only real stumbling block is fear of failure. In cooking you've got to have a what-the-hell attitude." –Julia Child

Most of us live busy lives, and it is more important than ever to create a loving, warm space for ourselves and our loved ones. A home can be one of life's greatest pleasures, a warm place for friends and family, and a refuge from the noisy demanding world.

Paula said that after her operation, she loved the two-week recuperation period, because for the first time in a long while, she had her girl friends over for lunch. Some of us are gifted in the art of homemaking, and others of us, learn as we go. In our modern society the homemaker is taken for granted. Yet it is what many of us yearn for in our lives: well-prepared, freshly cooked meals, clean orderly rooms, and time to visit with friends and families. When we learn to make time and space for home life and activities, we will be richly rewarded with a sense of balance that can carry us through the long days out in the world.

Chart 16 with its combination of home arts reminds us what to focus upon what is important.

Suggested Questions to Ask
- How can I make my home life better?
- How can I make all of us happier?
- What do I want to focus on?
- What would be nurturing for me?

Home Problem Solving (Chart 17)

A man travels the world over in search of what he needs and returns home to find it.–George Moore

In some ways a home is like a small service business. You have a physical plant to take care of; routine duties and responsibilities; and a budget. With a variety of tasks to perform and a sometime "volunteer" pool of workers it can seem impossible to keep it clean, with food on the table, seven days a week. Chart 19 will aid you in finding further solutions.

Suggested Questions to Ask
- What is the problem?
- What is the solution?
- What can I do to improve home life?
- What can all of us do together?

Gardening (Chart 18)

Gardening is food for the soul. –Kyra Eichhorn, Artist, Clairvoyant, and Teacher

For the green and non-green thumbed alike, Chart 18 helps you focus on creating your own special garden. Helping nature create her beauty can be healing to many hearts. Even that lowly activity, weeding, can be restorative on a sunny, spring day. Nature's variety, cyclical timing and generative abundance can serve as an example for our own lives and work.

Sally, a depressed, unemployed technology worker, was working with the charts. Though she was not a gardener by nature, she was surprised when the pendulum swung to the Gardening Chart, and then to *Bulbs*. She had forgotten she had bought a bag of daffodil bulbs the year before, but hadn't found the time to plant them. She spent an hour in her front yard with a shovel and trowel digging in the wet earth. Later that March when coming home from her new job, she noticed the first daffodil and other new green shoots.

What could you plant today that will bloom in six months?

Suggested Questions to Ask
- What would be healing to my heart and soul?
- What does the garden need?
- What else could I focus on?

Personal Finances (Chart 19)

Show me the money. –Cameron Crow, screenwriter, from the movie, Jerry McGuire

Where does your money come from? Your job, investments, or perhaps if you are lucky, an inheritance? Most of us work to create the money we live on; and, we are in a consumer society where we have been taught to buy and purchase happiness. As a nation, this attitude has led us not to freedom and joy, but to burden and enslavement.

And where does the money go? Because of our spending habits, many of us fritter away money that could be used for investment. Instead of peace of mind, we have credit card debt. By the time we reach the ripe age of thirty or forty, most of us have learned these painful lessons and have become a bit wiser.

So what is the solution? First, attempt to get honest with yourself. Use Chart 19 to ask where your major pitfalls are: Is it fear that you will never have enough coupled with a shopping addiction? Or is it a negative belief that you don't deserve peace of mind and a healthy financial future?

Whether we know it or not, we do have a relationship with money. Let yourself explore this arena of your life. Start by using this chart and its suggestions.

Suggested Questions to Ask
- What do I honesty need to know about myself?
- What is the problem?
- What is the solution?
- How do I improve my relationship with money?
-

Healing Arts (Chart 20)
As our lives unfold, our biological health become a living, breathing biographical statement that conveys our strengths, weaknesses, hope and fears. --Carolyn Myss, Ph.D.

We are so fortunate to live an open society where there is help for every human challenge, whether it be a communication issue or a drinking problem. We are no longer stigmatized for reaching out and finding help. We all will need help sometime in our lives. You can reduce the time you spend in a problem, sometimes cut it in half, just by reaching out.

Kathy and Claire were practicing with the charts together. Using the pendulum, they did mini-readings on each other and were directed to the Healing Arts Chart. Kathy was told she needed a Twelve Step group, as well as healthy eating habits. She had attended Overeaters Anonymous (OA) before, but hadn't been to a meeting in a year. Claire needed exercise for her well being and decided to join a gym. Now the two friends are supporting each other by attending OA together, eating well and going to the gym. That's what friends are for!

(Seek medical help if you have a physical problem. These charts are to be used in conjunction with proper medical treatments, to help you come into balance in your life.)

Suggested Questions to Ask
- What will help me with this issue?
- Is there any thing else I need to know?

Life Transitions (Chart 21)
Never think that God's delays are God's denials. Hold on; hold fast; hold out. Patience is genius. –Comte de Buffon

Change comes in all sizes. If unwanted and/or sudden, such as a divorce or job loss, we can find ourselves floundering in our emotional and financial lives. We can either fight or learn to flow with life and its transitions. Change of any kind whether we initiate it or not, can help us grow emotionally and spiritually, thus offering new, and perhaps unexpected, opportunities. When we find ourselves in the hallway it is important to remember, this situation will not last forever. We have choices.

Suggested Questions to Ask:
- What do I need?
- What do I want?
- How do I get out of the hallway?
- Where is the window? Where is the door?
- What is next?

Letting Go and Death (Chart 22)
The report of my death was an exaggeration. -Mark Twain

When confronted by illness or death, most of us will experience waves of overwhelming feelings – shock, fear, anger, and loss. The tools of Chart 22 offer solace and hope through the illness, grieving and dying process whether it is for ourselves or a loved one. Use what comforts and works best for you.

Moving through an illness or the death of a loved one is an aspect of life that we must all face. At times the process can seem like a harsh, painful teacher. Yet this is a time, if we allow it, that will open our hearts to help us find inner resources of courage, faith, forgiveness, and love, that perhaps we did not know we possessed. Fear of the unknown can lessen as we learn to live with our own mortality.

Suggested Questions to Ask
- What is needed?
- What am I afraid of?
- What do I need to complete?

Your Own Chart (Chart 23)

Only those who attempt the absurd, can achieve the impossible. –Sharon Schuster

Chart 23 will help you name and discover your own solutions to life's dilemma. Feel free to copy, and use it for whatever situation may arise.

You will realize when creating a new chart that you had more choices than you originally thought possible. Use your analytical skills to create a preliminary list, and your creative skills to enlarge on the solutions. Then create focus questions, and let the pendulum guide you to the answers.

Fun and Adventure (Chart 24)

If you postpone the journey until the storm passes, we may never get started. –J.I. Packer

When was the last time you allowed yourself to have an adventure? Sometimes we get so caught up in our responsibilities that we forget life can be a quest. If we can add spice and sport to our lives, we will be more committed to stay in the game longer.

Fun can make even the most difficult days bearable, and the good days better. If you find yourself having too little fun and becoming boorishly serious, Chart 24 is for you. Use your pendulum to discover how to improve your mood. Your children, spouse, friends, and co-workers will appreciate you more for boosting their day too.

Suggested Questions to Ask
- How can I have fun?
- How can I lighten up at home? At work?
- What would be good for my family?
- What else is needed?
- What would I love to do?
- What adventure can I plan for my life?

Prosperity Problem Solving (Chart 25)

The basic secret of unlimited supply is this: God is the source of man's supply, and He has provided many channels through which the riches of the universe can flow to him.
--Catherine Ponder, Secret of Unlimited Prosperity

We become disconnected from the truth of our being that *we are a part of this abundant, rich universe* by a block in our minds and emotions that prevents us from receiving the goodness we want and deserve.

The idea of lack comes first in our ego-minds telling us we are isolated beings; that there is nothing greater than our own thoughts, and that we must do it all ourselves if we are to make it in this random, impersonal universe.

Nothing could be further from the truth.

The thought-life of people is what draws to us what we have or do not have in our lives. After clearing the limited and fearful mind of its twisted thought forms, we can replace negativity with Truth by using affirmation, prayer, or meditation on who and what we truly are: *Divine Beings Living in an Abundant Universe.* And then, by focusing on our desires, we draw that which we truly want in life. This is where the "creator" in us meets the "Creator of the Universe."

To experience the fabric of a greater reality, it takes just a small adjustment in our thinking. We need simply to open the door of possibility and walk outside the small ego mind to meet the Higher Self, and God. This is where we can experience the web of life, our natural state of awareness, which is peaceful, loving, and creative.

When we begin taking responsibility for our thoughts and emotions, we realize we are creating much of the good and the difficult in our lives. We then get to examine our thoughts, beliefs and feelings, and choose more creative thoughts that allow us to manifest the life we desire.

Prosperity is defined as a flourishing or thriving condition. When used with the pendulum, The Prosperity Chart helps clear ourselves from what is blocking our ability to receive; and secondly, it helps expand prosperity in all aspects of our lives.

Have your desires eluded you? Use Chart 25 to clear your mind and emotions, and to assist you in creating all that you want in life.

Suggested Questions to Ask
- What would be helpful right now?
- What obstacles do I need to face?
- What needs to be cleared?
- What else do I need to do to open to prosperity?

Chapter 4
Delve Deeper
Inner Mapping Exercises
We learn the rope of life by untying its knots. ¬Jean Toomer

In this chapter, there are five Inner Mapping Exercises to help you gain self-knowledge. Some of these exercises allow you to learn more about your inner landscape, while others assist and direct your outer life. This chapter is about moving forward.

Included are the following:
• Past Life Issues and Solutions
• Qualities of the Inner Self
• The Shadow Self
• Control Issues
• The Quest for the Hero Within

Past Life Issues and Solutions
Sometimes we are held back by a challenge from a past life. Give yourself time and privacy to do the following powerful, healing process exercise. You may not believe in reincarnation, but for those of who do, and are curious, use the questions to begin research. Clear past lives using the pendulum and the Table of Charts I.(Be sure to take notes, so you can later reflect on the reading as a whole.)
  • What is the issue?
  • Is this a past life issue?
  • Who was it with? (Father, mother, brother, religious figure?)
  • How many lives did I have with this person?
  • Is this person in my life now?
  • Was there any harm done? Physical, emotional, psychological, spiritual?
  • What needs to be forgiven?
  • What belief needs to be let go?
  • What belief do I need to replace it with?
  • How do I forgive?
  • How do I heal?
  • What did I learn?

Qualities of the Inner Self
This exercise is illuminating. Jody, an artist, was able to clearly see the difference between what her "ego self" wanted versus what her Higher Self wanted. The ego self wanted Jody to be cool, smart, and funny while her Higher Power wanted her to be intelligent, loving, confident, forgiving,

relaxed, creative, and fully alive." Jody's Higher Power clearly had a bigger picture of her than she had of herself!

Use the pendulum and Intuitive Charts to answer the questions:
- Who would my ego self like me to be?
- Who do I think I am?
- Who would my Higher Self like me to be?
- Who am I?

In a short meditation, ask that your Higher Self take away all that is not truly who you are. Then see yourself as empty, and being filled with all that your Higher Self would like you to be. Breathe in and see these qualities sinking into your organs and bones, into every cell of your body.

The Shadow Self

Whom among us in our own actions or reactions to stressful events have not anguished? For instance, instead of being the kind and loving mom or dad we thought we were, we find ourselves raging at our small child. This other self seems to spring forth without warning.

The shadow, a term coined by Carl Jung, represents the aspects of our personalities that we project onto others. We prefer to think we are mature and grown up, but an "evil twin" sometimes lurks inside as a part of ourselves that we have discounted and disowned.

We can get away with blaming others, until one day it dawns on us that we are the common denominator. Surprise. None of us are perfect. Awareness is the anecdote to the shadow. By taking this inventory, and then claiming, clearing and releasing your shadow, you can make great strides in becoming the person you have always wanted to be.

Suggested Questions to Ask
- What do I fear?
- What do I hate in myself?
- What do I hate in others?
- What am I envious of?
- What am I afraid of?
- What shadow beliefs do I need to release?

When you are finished, close your eyes and breathe deeply. Ask for spiritual help to remove the pain and sadness, to clear the fear and hatred. Ask to forgive yourself and others. See Spirit pulling up the deep-seated beliefs, fears, and hatreds, then burning them in a bon fire. Soon there are just ashes and a feeling of forgiveness. Breathe deeply again and return your consciousness to the room feeling refreshed and free.

Control Issues

An excellent exercise is to make two lists: the people and things you have control over, and those you have no control over.

Control over this Person, Place, or Thing	No Control over this Person, Place, or Thing
_____	_____
_____	_____
_____	_____
_____	_____
_____	_____
_____	_____
_____	_____
_____	_____
_____	_____

Look at the first list. Put a plus by the things and situations you like, a star by the people you love. How can you increase the things you like? How can you spend more time with and give more to the people you love?

Put a minus sign in front of the things you don't like; and, find a way to let go of this energy drain.

For instance, at the top of my list of what I cannot control is other people. We can never truly change another human being; we cannot improve the spouse or a co-worker. We cannot force people to do things our way; at least not without serious consequences.

For those people, places, or things you cannot control, *I now give you permission to stop,* which is a precious waste of your positive energy.

The Quest for the Hero Within

Sometimes it is easier to find the inner shadow, than the hero, but there he is, larger than life! Or the heroine, waiting to solve human-made problems with her swift mind, her courageous heart, and get-it-done attitude. Ask the following questions to find your inner hero or heroine.

How do I make a difference in the lives of
- Family members?
- Work colleagues?
- Friends?
- Church?
- Community?
- Nation and world?

After checking the charts for answers, spend time meditating. Ask your spiritual guides for other ways to contribute and write down the responses. You will then notice how much you do give to the world.

Chapter 5
Give the Gift
of an Intuitive Reading

Let no one come to you without leaving better and happier. –Mother Theresa

I had recently begun coaching Liz, a beautiful mother, who was looking for more direction in her life. After two meetings, in which she had made profound progress deciding to pursue her love of art while raising her young children, she asked me if I would come to her home and do readings for each member of her family. Always up for a new adventure, I agreed to go.

A week later I drove up the coast on a rainy, fall afternoon. I was invited upstairs to a room overlooking the roaring ocean. As I coached Liz's mother and father, sister and brother-in-law, as well as her husband, this remarkable family intrigued me. Each of these individuals was deeply engaged in their home, business, and community lives. Two lawyers, a professional artist, a retired businessman, and a successful real estate developer and builder.

I began each session with a short centering prayer asking for spiritual guidance, clarity, and healing on any and all issues that might be revealed. As usual I explained the pendulum and charts process and listened to their life and business issues. As trust deepened, they relaxed and we were able to speak openly. I then clarified, cleared, and worked on healing the problems. The answers for each person began to flow.

Collectively, I used many of the Intuitive Charts – from the spiritual to transitions, and discussed love, past life, childhood, health, parenthood, right livelihood, partnering and business challenges. Delving deeply with each family member, we looked at these core issues. At the end I asked, "Do you have any more questions that you want to discuss?" As is inevitable, there were. Often the last question a client has been harboring is the one that needs to be examined and explored.

The final session was the longest. After finishing his reading, the practical, down-to-earth, get-it-done real estate developer wanted to know: "How does the pendulum work?" Within ten minutes he was able to move the pendulum.

Later, I received a call from Liz who said, "The shift in the entire family was subtle yet remarkable. The next morning everyone was more open and peaceful. We had a great, loving time together; and, they all want another session."

After the individual readings, each person was able to be authentic, present, and loving to one another. The power of the intuitive work to transform people's personal and business lives can happen in a few short hours.

Practice on Yourself First
A great person to practice giving Intuitive Readings on is you. You are available, willing, and you will be amazed at what you can discover. Or better yet, use the buddy system: learn with a friend, and practice giving Intuitive Readings to one another.

To begin, find a comfortable, private place. You may want to light a candle and say a prayer to create a sacred atmosphere. Give yourself a half-hour to an hour, so you have plenty of time to center, focus, and write down what you are learning.

Use the Free Form Reading Method in Chapter 1 or the more complete Intuitive Reading Worksheet found in this chapter. Keep the Worksheets in a notebook to track the progress you are making.

Before taking action with the insights you have received, check out your intuition with a friend, partner, or mentor. Ask someone who uses the pendulum and Intuitive Charts to verify your answers. The answers are to help you make decisions, but let your rational mind play its part too. This is a gentle, transformative system, allowing you to see all possibilities.

Then when you feel comfortable with your pendulum and Intuitive Chart use, you can give Intuitive Readings to family and/or friends.

Giving the Gift to Another
When offering Intuitive Readings to others, remember the purpose of the time spent together is to encourage the best in a person. Help them see a broader picture of their life and gently guide them in the direction they want to take. Let it be a positive, life affirming time that lifts you both to higher plane.

- Take a moment first to clear yourself and your client. Say an affirmation to call upon Spirit (choose whichever name of God or Spirit you feel comfortable with) to assist in the Reading. For instance, "We ask Spirit to guide and direct this Reading. Help us to clarify and to resolve these issues today. Thank you for your help and guidance."
- Listen closely to the person with both your mind and heart. Do not judge; instead listen carefully as they speak. Practice your active listening skills by repeating back to the speaker what you hear.
- Take brief notes on the issues and people that concern them. By writing a few notes, you will be more objective, less emotionally

involved; therefore, you will be able to direct the flow of the meeting. Don't get lost in the written details and forget to focus on your client. I use a handy clipboard with the Intuitive Reading Worksheet. You may want, make a copy for your client to help them process the Intuitive Reading.
- Take the time to help your friend or client clarify their issues and questions, so that when you use the pendulum and Intuitive Charts to research, your will receive clear answers.
- When you do the research with the pendulum and charts, tell them the answers, so they reach their own conclusions. To drill down to deeper levels, ask, "What does this mean for you?" Then you gently share your insights.
- Tell them the truth as you see it with love and compassion.
- Next, clear them and insert what will be healing to their mind, heart, and emotions. This is the most important step!
- At the end of the reading ask, "Do you have any further questions or concerns?"
- Always be a channel of Spirit's love, compassion, and forgiveness.
- Keep tissues handy.
- End with a prayer of thanks, knowing that Spirit has worked in your life as well as theirs. *As we give, so we receive.*
- After you are complete with the reading, clear yourself and wash your hands. Give yourself and your clients a few minutes to leave this sacred space and re-enter the world. Offer water and drink some yourself.
- Hold whatever is said during a reading in confidence.

Note: **Remember that you are not a doctor or therapist**. At times people with complex problems will arrive. Lovingly refer them to others with more experience: to a doctor, trained therapist, or other professional.

Two ways to do Readings:
- The Free Form Reading is a quick method to check for answers.
- The Intuitive Reading utilizes a worksheet and guides you through a complete process.

Free Form Reading
Create a question you wish to answer. Write it down for more clarity, and begin the following exercise.

- Start at either of the Table of Charts; ask your question while holding the pendulum over the circle in the center.
- The pendulum will begin moving toward the name of a chart. Go to this second chart and ask your question again.
- Write down your answers.

- When you have your answer or answers, return to the Table of Charts, and ask, "What else do I need?" Again you will be led to another chart.
- As this continues, return to the Table of Charts as many times as necessary.
- When you return to the Table of Charts and the pendulum stops moving, you know your question has been answered.

My friend Sally, who is funny, intelligent and beautiful, had the guts to leave a cute and sexy guy who didn't have the same goals as she. Sally was thirty-three and wanted to get married. A month into this enjoyable, but going nowhere romance, she knew he wasn't the one. Months later she told him the truth and they parted amicably. She did the following reading for herself.

Starting at the Relationship Chart, she asked these questions:
- Is anything blocking me from having a new relationship?
- What will help me?
- Is there anything else?

Her first answer was *Forgiveness*. She realized she had forgiven him, but not herself for ignoring the red flag she saw waving: On the first date he said he wasn't the marrying kind. Sally felt she had wasted months. Right then, she decided to forgive herself and get on with life. Sally was led to the answer, *Make a List*. She then wrote a detailed list of everything she wanted – magic, fun, beauty, honesty, and marriage. Back at the Relationship Chart, Sally was told to *Relax*. Four weeks later, she met a man who was athletic, smart, and fun who seemed like a good match. Soon after meeting him she used her pendulum to ask: "Should I date this man?" The answer was a loud *Yes*.

These are easy ways to coach yourself or a friend and to use the Intuitive Charts in deeper, more meaningful ways.

How to Use the Intuitive Reading Worksheet
Clear and center yourself before beginning. See the Intuitive Reading Worksheet. Scan these to get an understanding of the process and then walk yourself through until you get the knack of it. After completing a few readings on yourself and others you will be more comfortable and the information will flow. (Make copies of the Intuitive Reading Worksheet found in the Appendix for your own use.) This is a simple, but profound seven-step process.

Step One – State the Issues: Clarify what the real issue is and write about it as a list or a series of questions.

Step Two – Name the Person, Place, or Thing: Who and what is the issue with? For instance, is it a sister who calls ranting about her husband or an irritating co-worker? Check the Tables of Charts.

Step Three – Research: Begin by using general questions, such as,
- What do I need to know?
- What do I need to see?
- What is the underlying problem?
- What am I not seeing? (For example, is the problem with my sister or is it because I have poor boundaries and cannot tell her, *I need to go now.)*

Or use the Suggested Questions to Ask in the proceeding chapters. The more specific your questions, the better your answers will be. You will grow in this questioning skill as you gain experience.

Step Four – Find Solutions: Ask, "What are my options? What are the solutions? What would be best for me? What would be best for all concerned?"

Step Five – Clear: Go back to the Table of Charts and ask: What is needed to clear or heal this issue? You will be guided to an answer or answers. To clear the issue, ask Spirit simply to remove what is blocking you, and insert what will help you. For example if I found out that behind my anger was fear, I might say a short prayer like this: "In the name and through your power, I ask that fear be removed and replaced with love." Use the your pendulum and watch as your pendulum swings in a circular, clockwise direction to clear. When the pendulum stops you know you are cleared. Take your time to do this most important step.

Step Six – Take Action: Now, having a bigger picture of the problem, ask: What further actions can I take?

Step Seven – Write an Affirmation: Use Chart 10, Empowering Thoughts, to create an affirmation or a positive statement, that empowers you to accomplish what needs to be done. Write it in the present tense and include your name in the affirmation. End with a short prayer of thanks.

After doing a reading for yourself or another, it's a good idea to wash your hands and drink a cool, glass of water. Whether you realize it or not, you have been processing and healing deep thoughts and powerful emotions. Pause before you enter life again, take some deep breaths, and give thanks for all your blessings.

Intuitive Reading Worksheet

Name _____ **Date** _____

Step 1 – What is the issue? State the issue as clearly as possible.

Step 2 – Name the person, place or thing. Who or what is upsetting me?

Step 3 – Research – What do I need to know? What is the underlying cause?

Step 4 - Solutions - What are the solutions?

Step 5 - Clearing - Remember to clear self and/or others.

Step 6 – Action - What positive actions can I take?

Step 7 - What is my new belief? Write an affirmation to support the new belief.

David, an intelligent businessman, made an appointment with me out of curiosity. His life was going well, he was starting a second career, investing in the stock market, and he enjoyed a loving wife and his four grandchildren. David asked if I ever did past life readings. For years he had glimpses, visions, and sometimes dreams of a warrior life. As David was a very gentle man, he was somewhat bothered by these fierce images.

Checking the Time and Percent Chart (Chart 3) we found he had twelve or more lives as a warrior! I asked him if he would like to experience this in a short meditation. After a closing his eyes and taking a few relaxing breathes and a short visualization, David saw himself riding across a desert landscape, thundering on an Arabian horse, brandishing his sword. I asked him how he thought this applied to his life now and he said, "I am always cool under pressure, and objective, when work and life seems to be falling apart. People know they can depend on me."

Then I checked the Table of Charts I and was led to the People Chart (Chart 5), where the pendulum pointed to *Female*. When we checked we found he had many lives as a woman. I again asked if he wanted to experience this and again he said yes. David's initial sensation was that he was uncomfortable in a softer, rounder body. He disliked the feelings of powerlessness and limitation. I checked the Time and Percent Chart (Chart 3) and found it took five life times for him to get comfortable in the female body and role.

David, who left the session feeling as if he understood himself much better e-mailed me a few days later saying, "I felt as if I was given puzzle pieces of my own personal history. I have been pondering these visions of past lives. Generally, I just feel more at peace with myself and the direction my life is taking."

Whether you or giving yourself a reading, honor the time that you spend intuitively coaching yourself or others. Like David, you can discover your own inner male and female, your warrior, and you're nurturing selves.

The beauty of Intuitive Readings is that you quickly get to the heart of an issue, and by clearing and healing, you release and let a problem go. What you are giving is the experience of allowing others see life filled with more freedom, adventure, and possibility than they had previously believed.

In this moment you and all people are free to choose again. In the rhythm of life itself--with its continual cycle of birth, death, and rebirth--you can be guided by your inner self and Spirit to a new level of joy. Use these methods to give birth to yourself and others again and again. Remember: *the true power is within you.*

Epilogue
Transformation
The door to the world is the heart. – Corita Kent

Just as we awaken every morning and leave the world of our dreams, that non-linear, magic place where anything is possible, so too do we leave a meditative space to face home and work responsibilities. We then eat our breakfast, drive to work, and enter the more linear work and business worlds with their myriad of responsibilities and roles to enact.

With practice, the pendulum and Intuitive Charts begin to work in our lives. As we change inwardly, we manifest success in our outer lives; we remember to celebrate our wins and give thanks. We learn to take the ups and downs in stride using the Intuitive Tools for balance and integration as we move through life transitions.

We live one day at a time and we ask for spiritual help in moments of tension and crisis. We remind ourselves on our coffee breaks and on walks at lunch of our spiritual roots. We are careful to honor ourselves by using discretion with whom we share our new knowledge, making sure it is with people who are open to intuitive gifts.

In a sense we have our feet in two worlds. As Irene Claremont de Castillejo explains: "Only a few achieve the colossal task of holding together, without being lit asunder, the clarity of their vision alongside an ability to take their place in a materialistic world. They are the modern heroes. . ."

In the end, it is all about transforming your life so that you can be all you were meant to be. With Spirit's help, you participate in the re-creation of yourself. By living authentically, you help others to live from their true selves. *As one is transformed, so is another.* And so it goes. Know in the depths of your being that you are always taken care of in mind, spirit, and body. Go with great love and wisdom on this journey.

Intuitive Guidance + Action = Success

Bibliography/Suggested Readings

Creativity
Bryan, Mark with Julia Cameron, and Catherine Allen, *The Artists Way at Work*. New York, NY, Quill William Morrow, 1998.

Cameron, Julia with Mark Bryan, *The Artist Way*, New York, NY: G. P. Putnam, 1992.

Gawain, Shakti, *Creative Visualization*, New York, NY: Bantam Books, 1982.

Intuition
Frost, Seena B., *SoulCollage*, Santa Cruz, CA: Handford Mead Publishers, Inc., 2001.

Weintraub, Sandra, *The Hidden Intelligence: Innovation Through Intuition*, Tutterworth-Heinemann, 1998.

Wilde, Stuart, *Sixth Sense*, Carlsbad, CA: Hay House, 2000.

Finances
Allen, Marc, *The Millionaire Course: A Visionary Plan for Creating the Life of Your Dreams*, Novato, Ca: New World Library, 2003.

Kiyosaki, Robert, *Rich Dad, Poor Dad*, New York, NY: Warner Books, 1997.

Orman, Suze, *The 9 Steps to Financial Freedom*, New York, NY: Three Rivers Press, 1997.

Meditation
Butler-Ross, Nancy L. and Michael Suib, *Meditation Express*. Lincolnwood, IL: Contemporary Books, 2001.

Pendulum Methods
Detzler, Robert E., *The Freedom Path*, Snohomish, WA: Snohomish Publishing Company, Inc., 1996.

Detzler, Robert E., *Soul Recreation; Developing Your Cosmic Potential*, Redmond, WA: SRC Publishing revised 1999.

Jurriaanse, D., *The Practical Pendulum Book*, York Beach, ME: Samuel Weiser, Inc., 1986. Translated from the Dutch, published in Holland, 1984.

Lonegren, Sig, *The Pendulum Kit*, New York, NY: Simon & Schuster, 1990.

Nielsen, Greg and Polansky, Joseph, *Pendulum Power*, Rochester, VT: Destiny Books, 1977, 1987.

Webster, Richard, *Dowsing for Beginners*, St. Paul, MN: Llewellyn Publications, 2003.

Prosperity

Chopra, Deepak, *The Seven Spiritual Laws of Success*, San Rafael, CA:

Dyer, Wayne W., *Manifest Your Destiny*, New York, New York:
HarperCollins Publishers, 1997.

Ponder, Catherine, *Secret of Unlimited Prosperity*, Marina del Rey, CA:
DeVorss & Company, 1981.

Ritz, David Owen, *The Keys to the Kingdom*, David Owen Ritz, Chicago,
IL, 1998.

Spirituality

Bodin, Echo L., *A Still, Small Voice: A Psychic's Guide to Awakening
Intuition*, Novato, CA: New World Library.1999.

Course in Miracles, Tiburon, CA: Foundation for Inner Peace,1975.

Gawain, Shakti, *Living in the Light: A Guide to Personal and Planetary
Transformation*, Novato, Ca: Nataraj Publishing, a division of New
World Library, 1998.

Hiller, Margaret and David, *Dare to Dream*, Ashland, OR: Heart Dream
Press, 2002.

Ruiz, Don Miguel, *The Four Agreements*, San Rafael, CA: Amber-Allen
Publishing, Inc., 1997.

Virtue, Doreen, *The Lightworker's Way: Awakening Your Spiritual Power
to Know and Heal*, Carlsbad, CA: Hay House Inc., 1997.

Williamson, Marianne, *A Return to Love: Reflections on the Principles of "A
Course in Miracles"* New York, NY: HarperCollins, 1992.

Acknowledgments

I wish to thank the following people:

- Shakti Wilson, teacher, minister, and coach for her many hours of patiently working with me on so many different and varied levels.
- My children, Adam and Danielle, who have been so loving and encouraging during the past year when I wrote this book. They inspire me with their love, enthusiasm for life, and incredible talent, which I sometimes feel I inherited from them.
- My editor and writing coach, Kathleen Miller-Thomas, who patiently and quickly gave shape and form to my writing, who herself is a gifted writer, painter, and photographer and a delight to work with.
- To my courageous and remarkable clients who have taught me much, and who allowed me to use their stories.
- My team at JointSolutions Marketing who encouraged me and help create the book: Linda McDanel White, Alexa Keihl, Brian Morrisey, Scot McKenzie, Julie Triano, and Richard McKenzie.
- The inventive Connie Strawbridge for her artistry and the creative Will Northcutt for ideas and art direction.
- My sisters, who have walked with me on this sometimes onerous, but ultimately joyful life path. Theresa Moldvay, Laurie Carah, and Leslie Torvik.
- All my courageous, encouraging women friends: Kyra Eichhorn, Vickie Assunto, Jackie Lenway Leppla, Carol Pavlina, Kimberlee Kay, Shauna Gunderson, my first writing teacher, Ellen Bass and her women's "Writing for Your Lives" group, Valerie White, my gifted psychic and friend, Debi Derham, my massage therapist, Lara Sprinkles, my Flower Essence Teacher, all who supported my efforts day after day, and month after month.
- Robert and Marianne Dexler, and their *Spiritual Response Therapy System* (SRT) for establishing a wonderful new way to help heal people and spiritually transform their lives.
- Unity Temple of Santa Cruz and the Association of Unity Churches for my best spiritual training.
- All of the authors of the books I have read and used over the years that have continually inspired me and helped change my life.
- God/Goddess, Jesus, Mary Magdalene, James Staffen, the Angels of Light and Love, and all those on the other side who assist in our transformative, earthly work.

Appendix
The Foundation and Personal Charts

Foundation Charts – *Decision Making, Issues, and Thoughts*

Yes/No and Clearing (Chart 1)

Think and Act (Chart 2)

Time and Percent (Chart 3)

Primary Issues (Chart 4)

People (Chart 5)

Seek and Find Spirit (Chart 6)

Spiritual Guides (Chart 7)

Spiritual Tools (Chart 8)

Limited Thoughts (Chart 9)

Empowering Thoughts (Chart 10)

Blessings (Chart 11)

Personal Charts –*Love, Home & Life Issues*

Love and Romance (Chart 12)

Nurturing Relationships (Chart 13)

Parenting (Chart 14)

Feelings (Chart 15)

Home Arts & Responsibilities (Chart 16)

Home Problem Solving (Chart 17)

Gardening (Chart 18)

Personal Finances (Chart 19)

Healing Arts (Chart 20)

Life Transitions (Chart 21)

Letting Go & Death (Chart 22)

Your Own Chart (Chart 23)

Fun & Adventure (Chart 24)

Prosperity Problem Solving (Chart 25)

Before beginning: center yourself, take a few deep breaths and ask using your pendulum:

- Am I working with my Higher Self?
- Are my answers 100% accurate?

If the answer is no, keep clearing until you are ready.

If you are working on another person, always ask first:

- Do I have permission to work on this person?
- Is this for the highest good for this person?

If an answer is no, say a prayer for them, and place them in Spirit's hands.

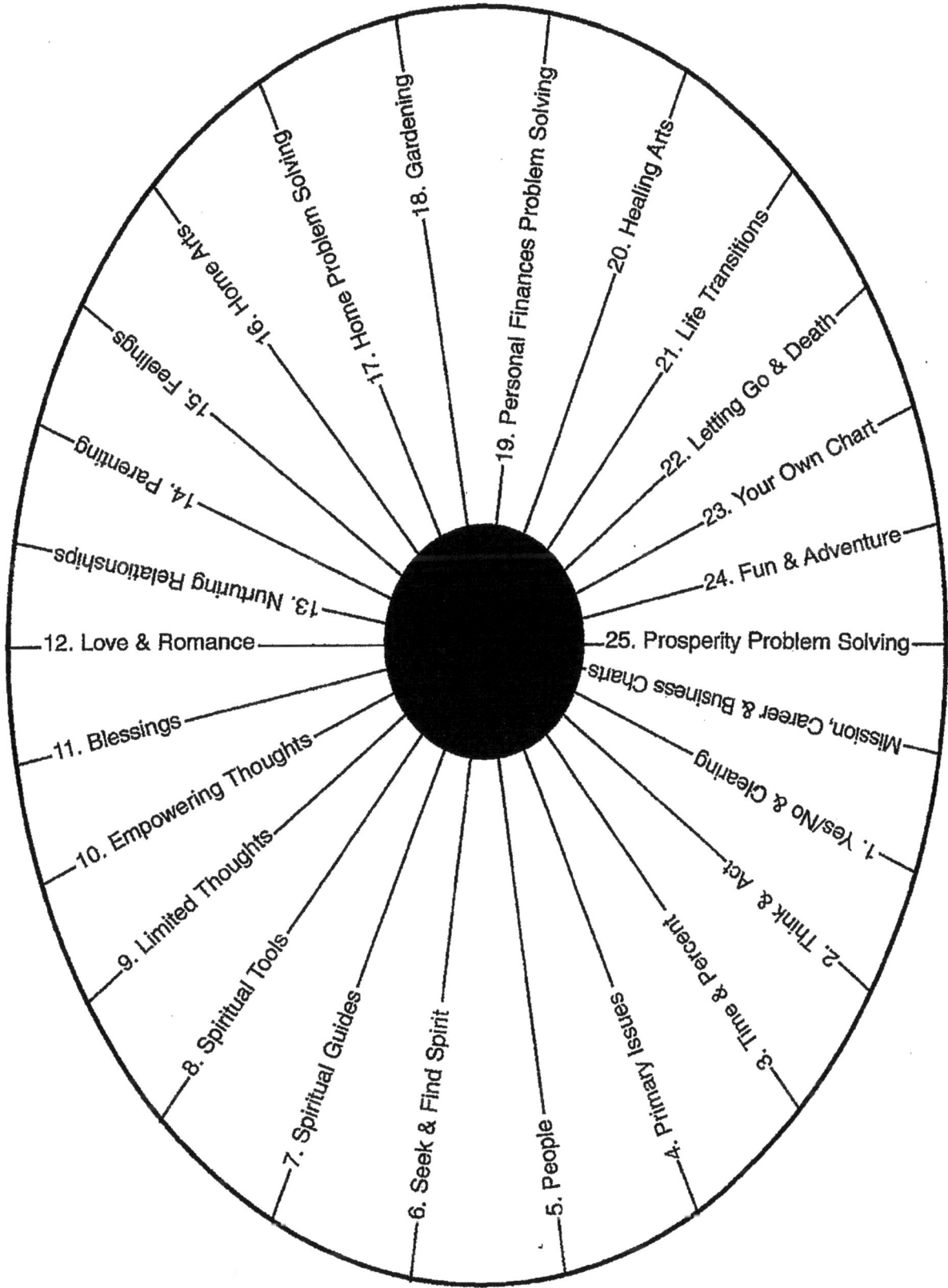

Foundation and Personal Charts
(Table of Charts I)

1. Yes/No & Clearing
2. Think & Act
3. Time & Percent
4. Primary Issues
5. People
6. Seek & Find Spirit
7. Spiritual Guides
8. Spiritual Tools
9. Limited Thoughts
10. Empowering Thoughts
11. Blessings
12. Love & Romance
13. Nurturing Relationships
14. Parenting
15. Feelings
16. Home Arts
17. Home Problem Solving
18. Gardening
19. Personal Finances Problem Solving
20. Healing Arts
21. Life Transitions
22. Letting Go & Death
23. Your Own Chart
24. Fun & Adventure
25. Prosperity Problem Solving
Mission, Career & Business Charts

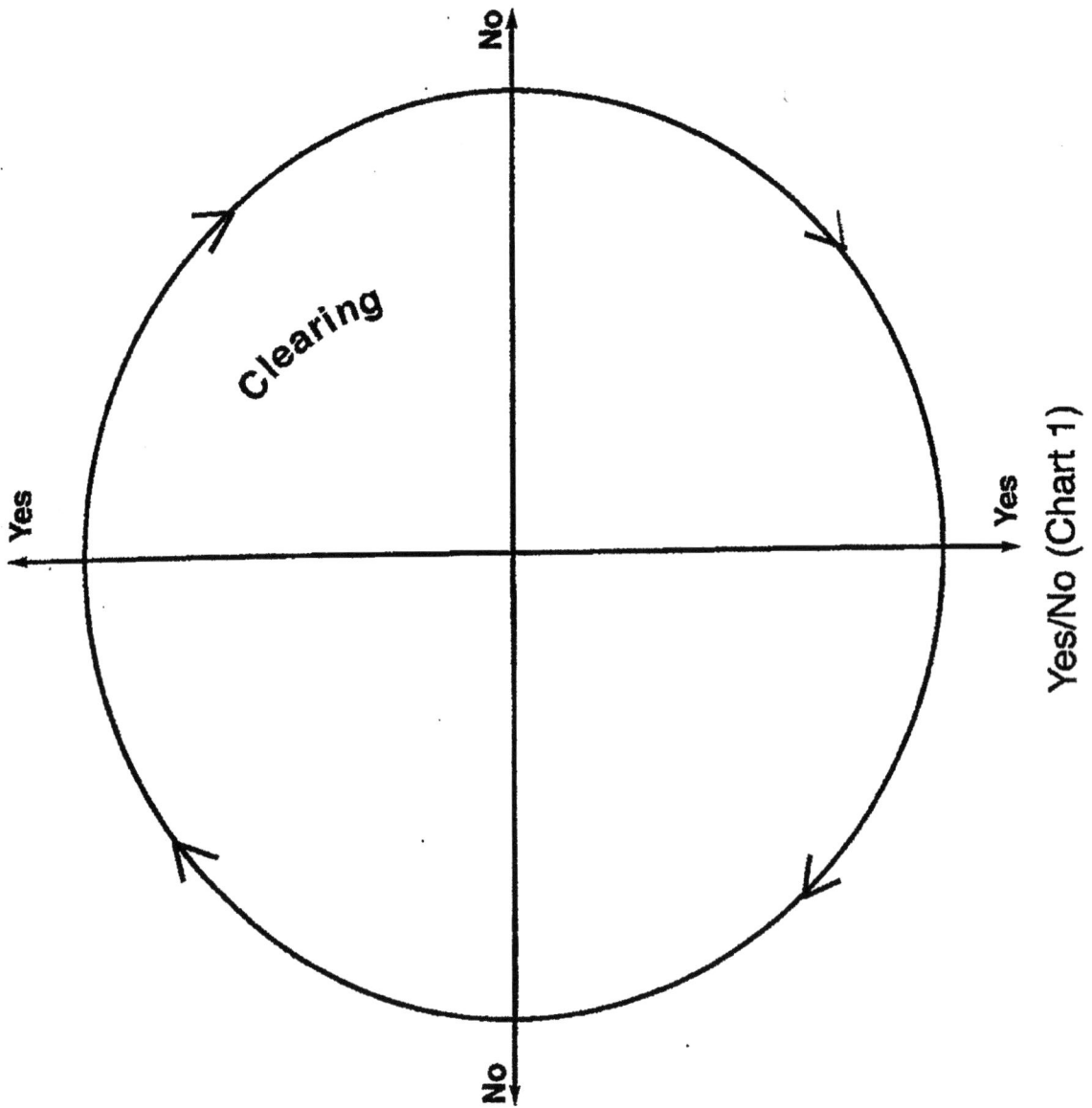

No

Clearing

Yes

Yes/No (Chart 1)

Yes

No

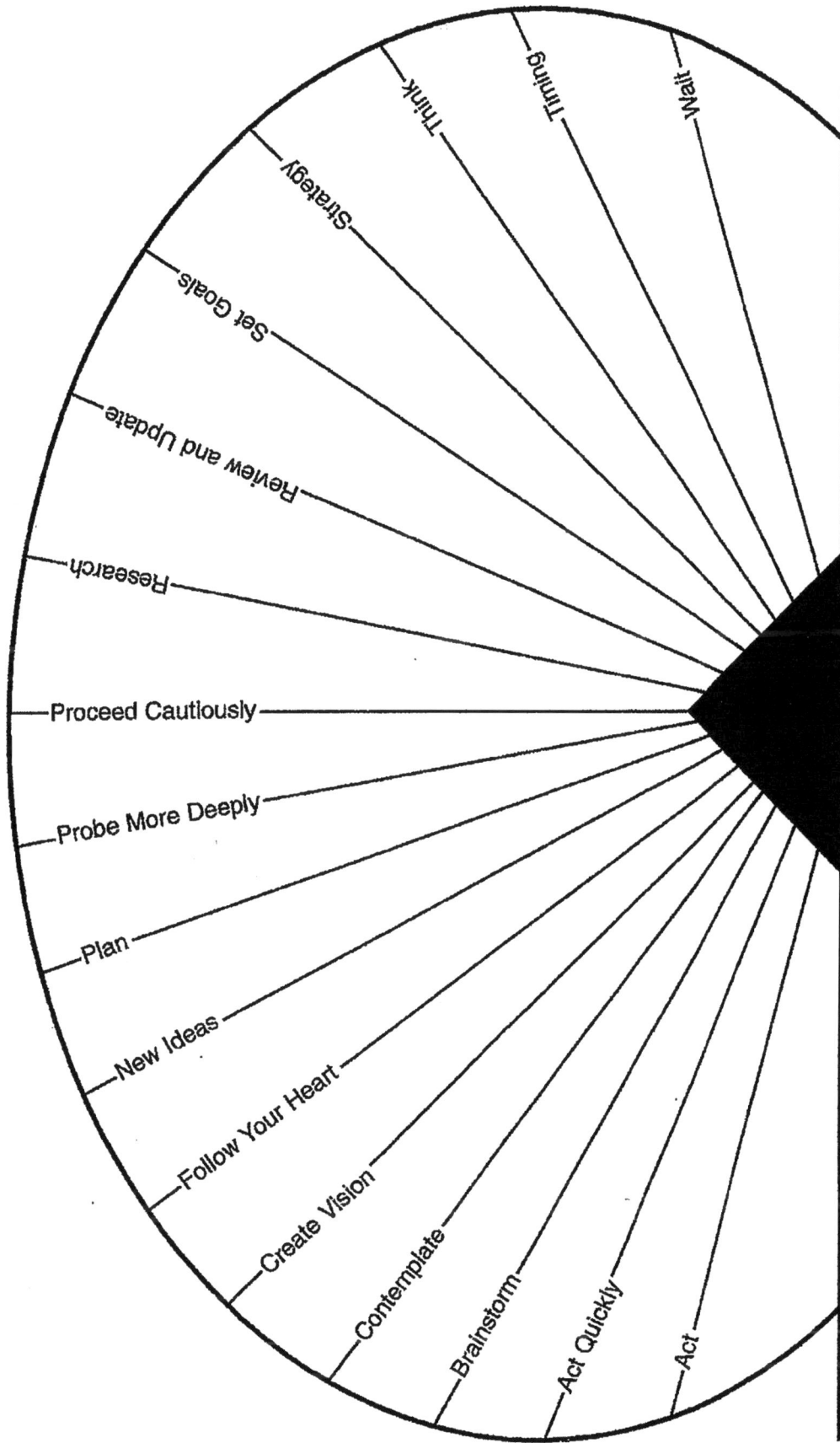

Think and Act (Chart 2)

- Wait
- Timing
- Think
- Strategy
- Set Goals
- Review and Update
- Research
- Proceed Cautiously
- Probe More Deeply
- Plan
- New Ideas
- Follow Your Heart
- Create Vision
- Contemplate
- Brainstorm
- Act Quickly
- Act

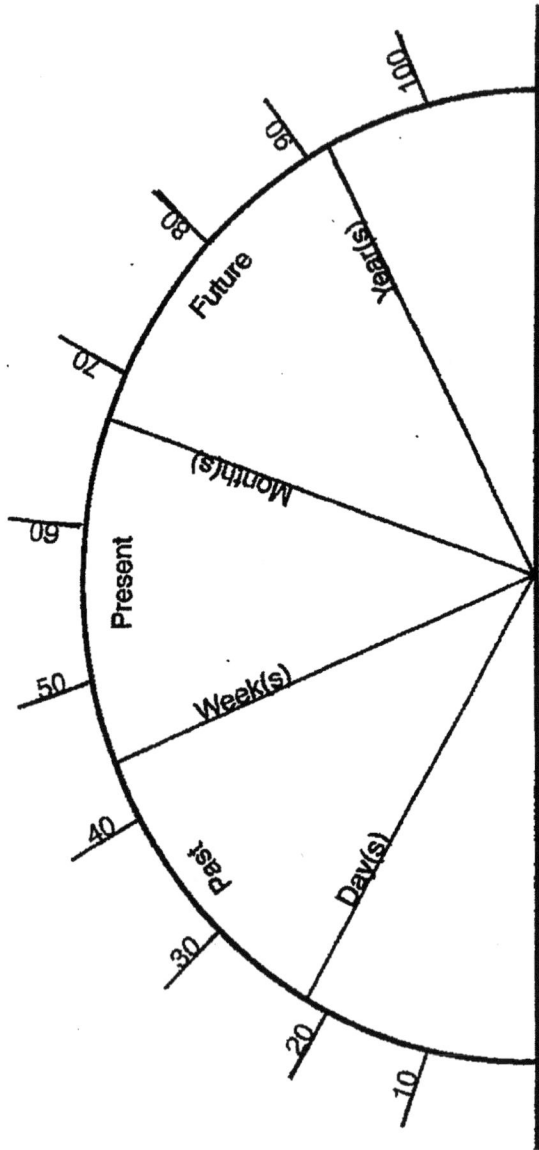

Time & Percent (Chart 3)

Future

Present

Past

Year(s)

Month(s)

Week(s)

Day(s)

100
90
80
70
60
50
40
30
20
10

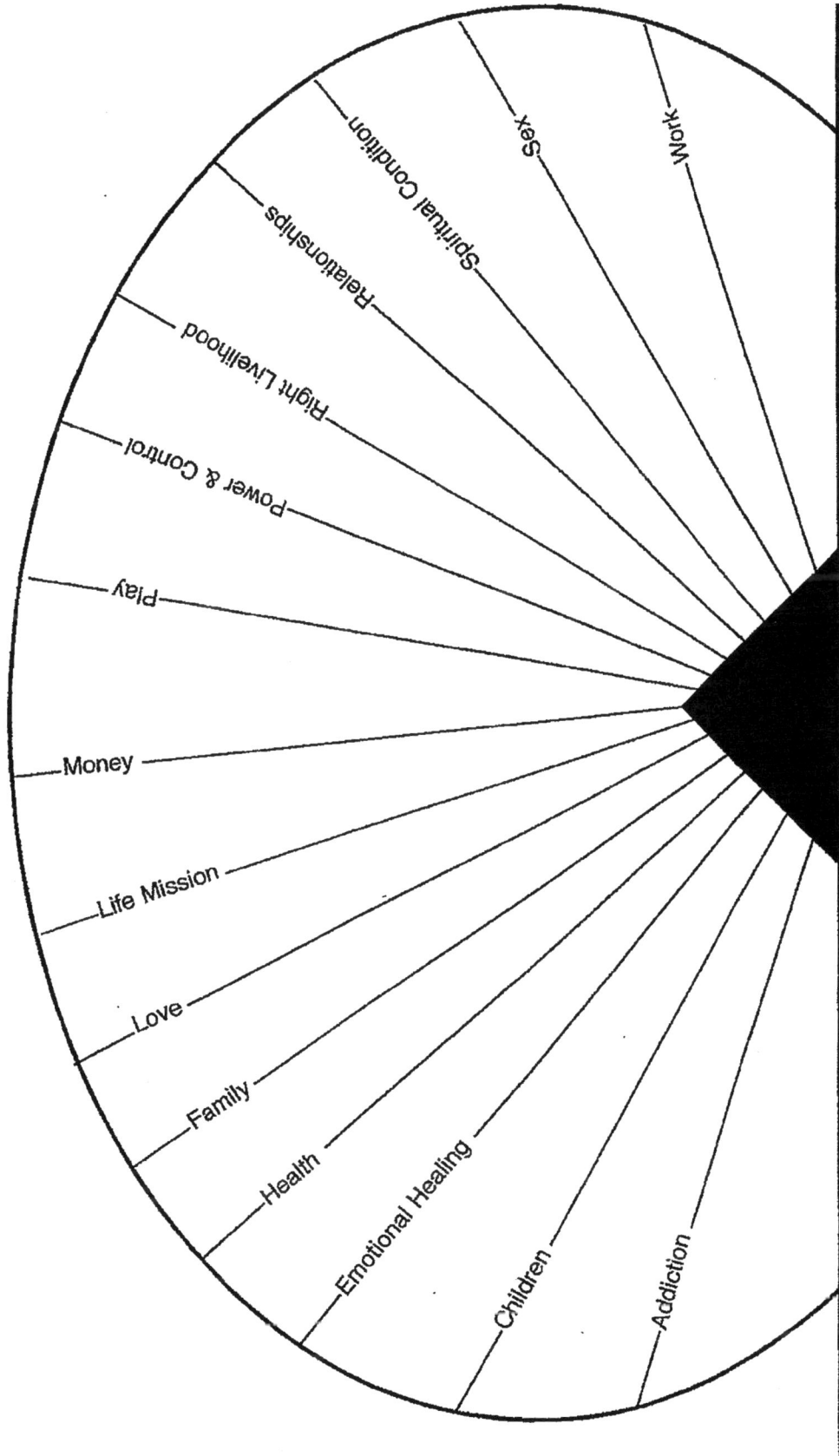

Primary Issues (Chart 4)

- Work
- Sex
- Spiritual Condition
- Relationships
- Right Livelihood
- Power & Control
- Play
- Money
- Life Mission
- Love
- Family
- Health
- Emotional Healing
- Children
- Addiction

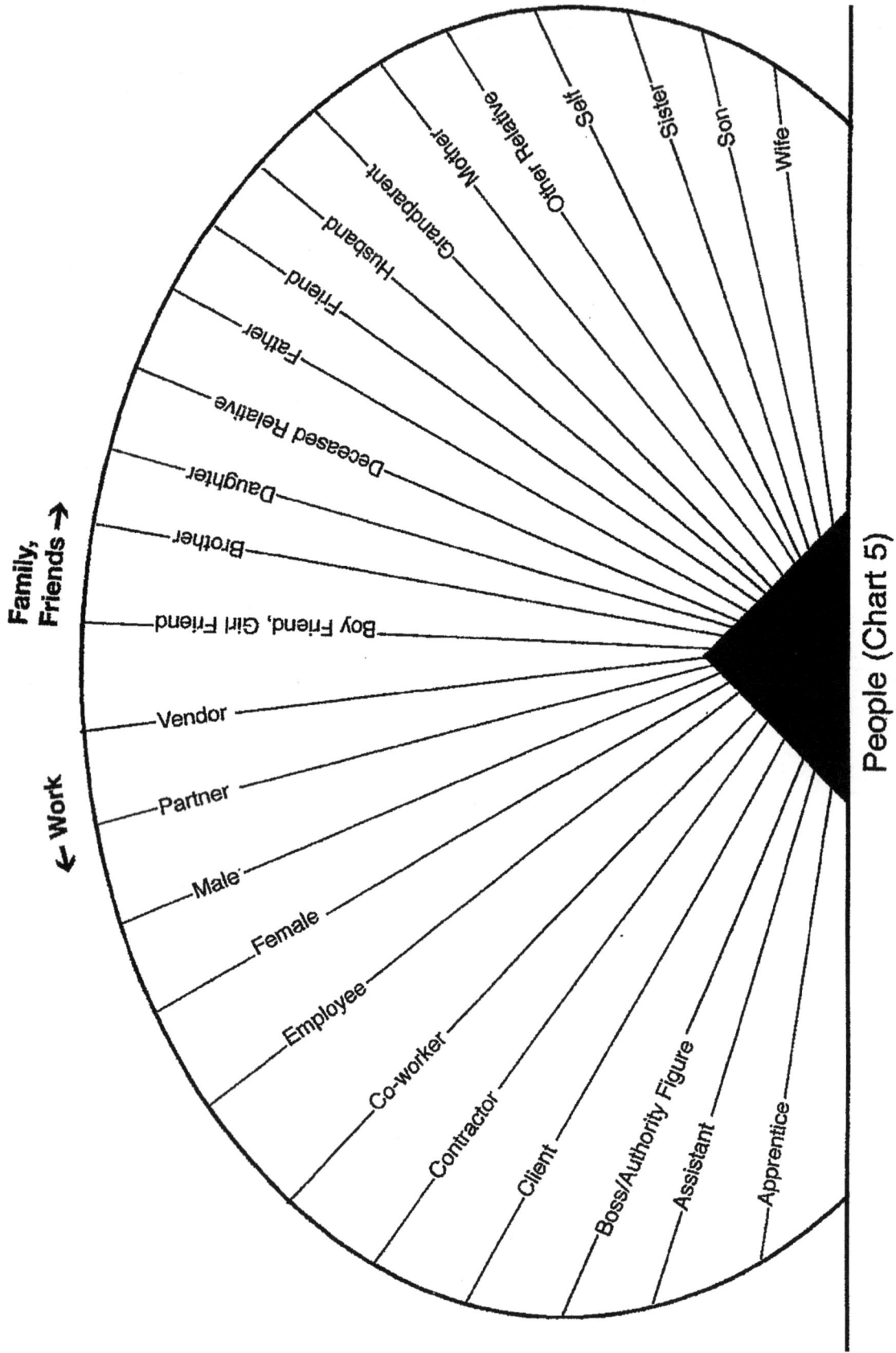

People (Chart 5)

Family, Friends →

← Work

- Wife
- Son
- Sister
- Self
- Other Relative
- Mother
- Grandparent
- Husband
- Friend
- Father
- Deceased Relative
- Daughter
- Brother
- Boy Friend, Girl Friend
- Vendor
- Partner
- Male
- Female
- Employee
- Co-worker
- Contractor
- Client
- Boss/Authority Figure
- Assistant
- Apprentice

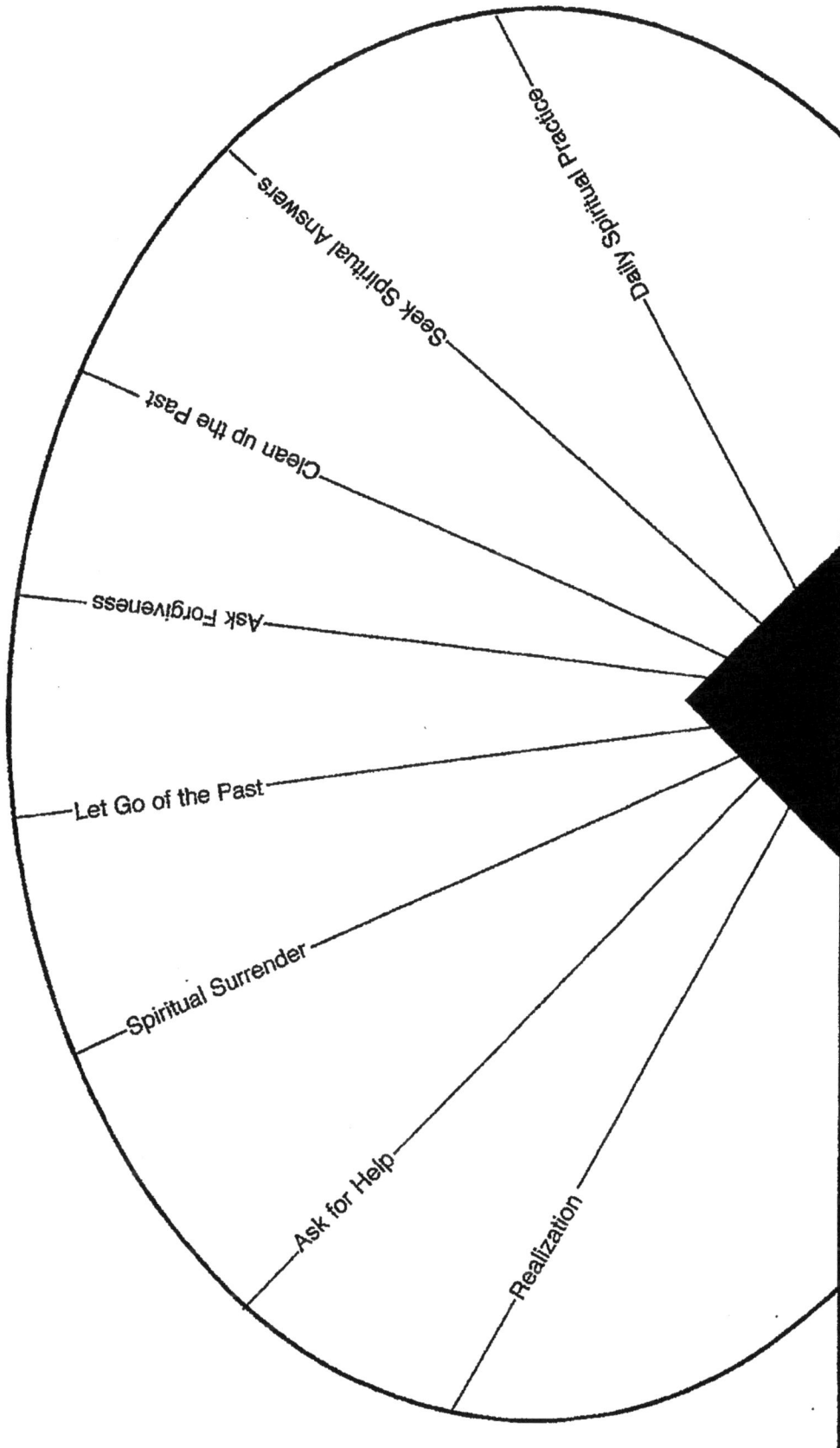

Seek & Find Spirit (Chart 6)

Daily Spiritual Practice

Seek Spiritual Answers

Clean up the Past

Ask Forgiveness

Let Go of the Past

Spiritual Surrender

Ask for Help

Realization

Spirit

Muhammad

Jesus & Mary

High Self

Higher Power

Guide

Great Spirit

God/Goddess

Fairy

Ego

Deceased
Loved One

Counselor

Buddha

Ascended Master

Angel

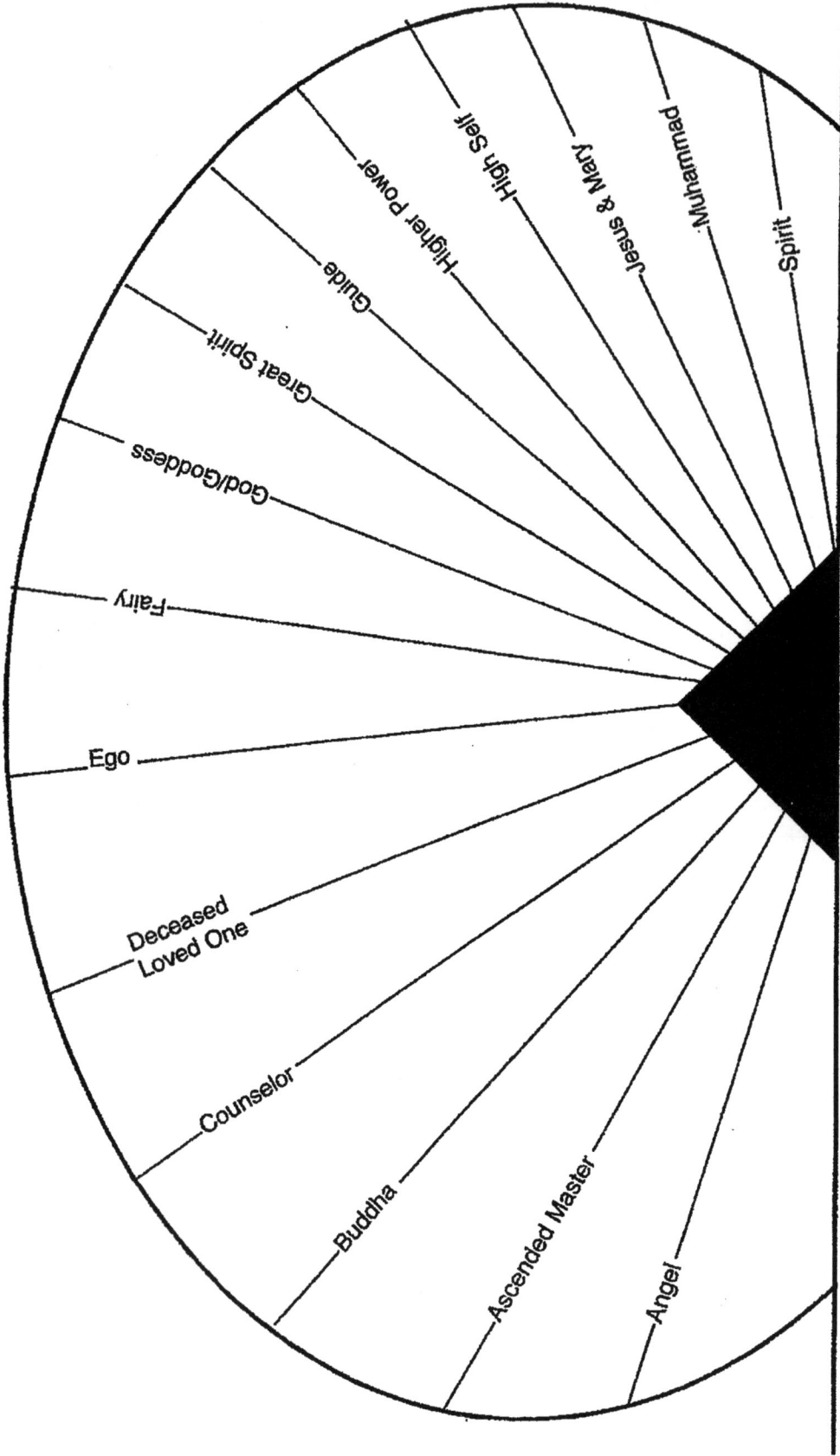

Spiritual Guides (Chart 7)

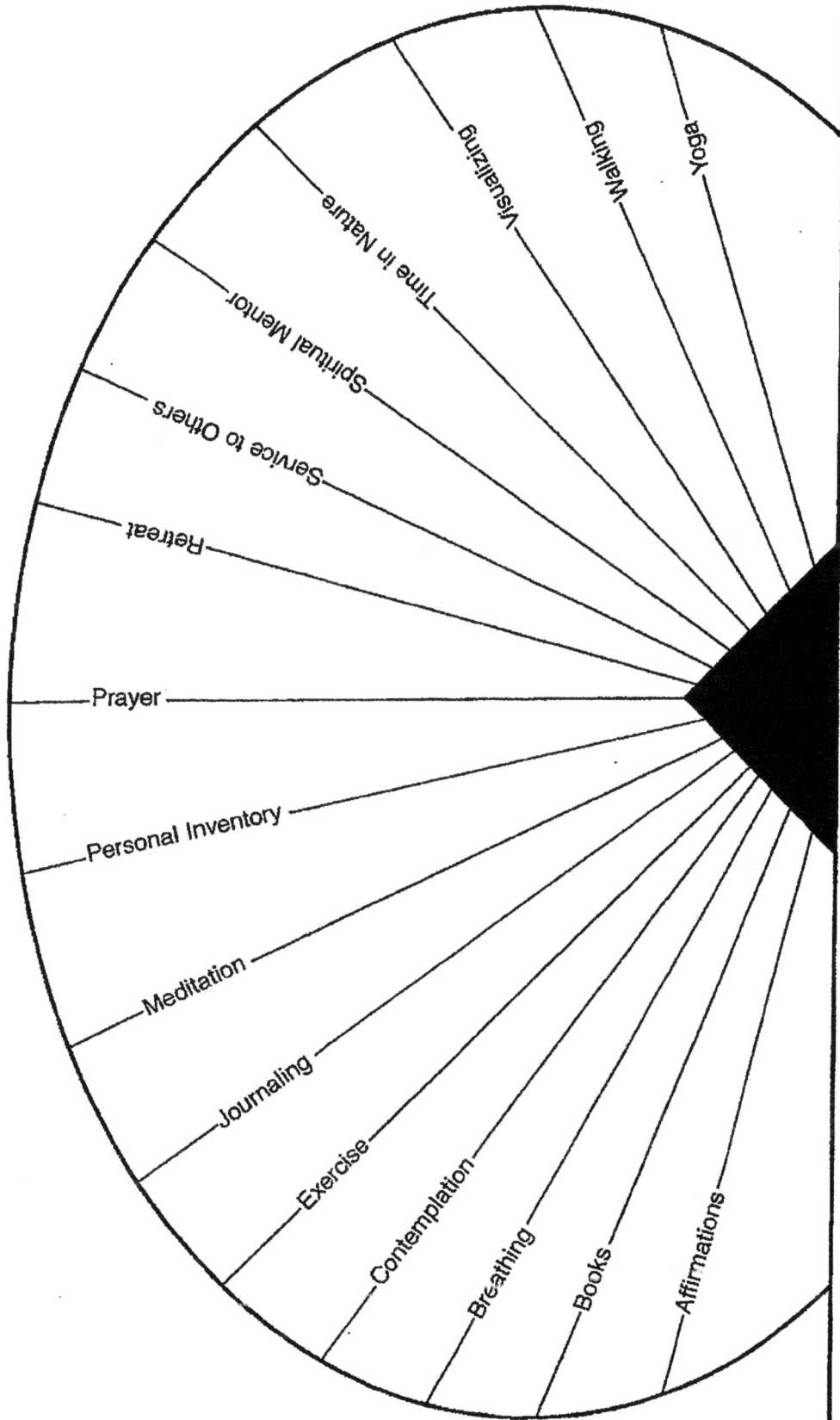

Spiritual Tools (Chart 8)

- Yoga
- Walking
- Visualizing
- Time in Nature
- Spiritual Mentor
- Service to Others
- Retreat
- Prayer
- Personal Inventory
- Meditation
- Journaling
- Exercise
- Contemplation
- Breathing
- Books
- Affirmations

Resistance

Lethargy

Laziness

Lying

Jealousy

Insecurity

Injustice

Hate

Greed

Fear of Success

Fear of Relationship

Fear of Failure

Fear of Authority

Fear

Doubt

Depression

Conflict

Betrayal

Appeasement

Anger

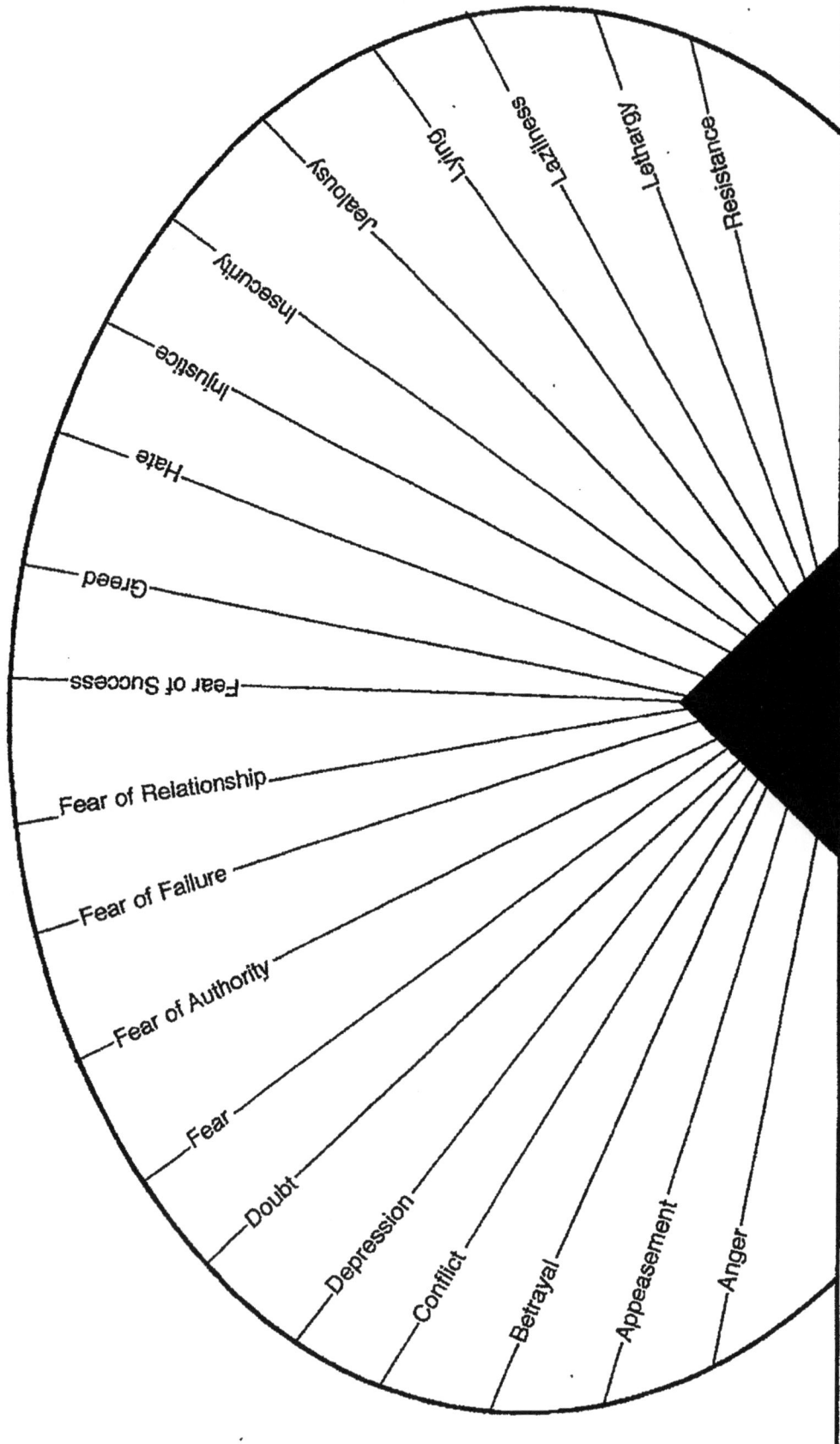

Limited Thoughts (Chart 9)

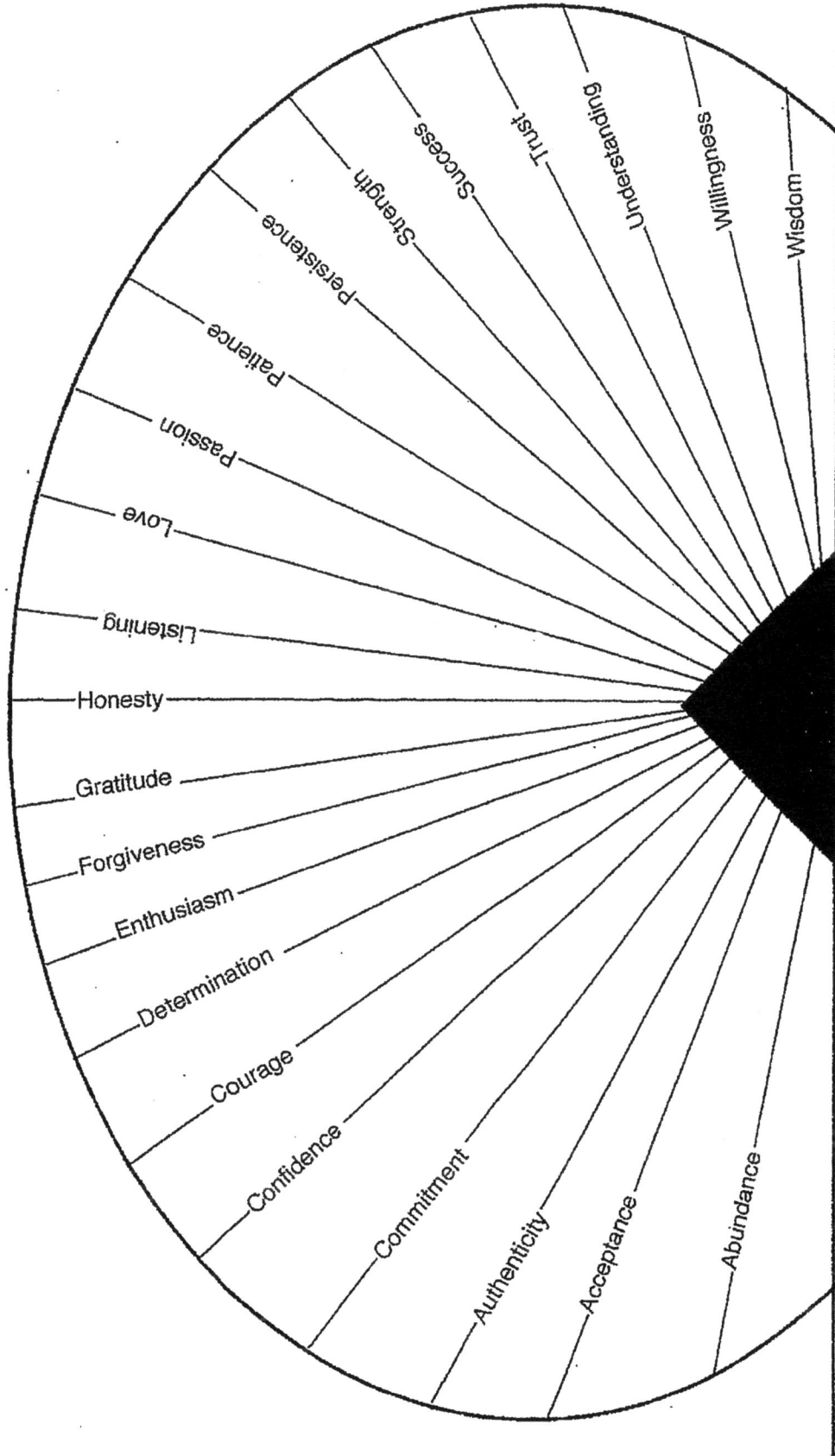

Empowering Thoughts (Chart 10)

Wisdom
Willingness
Understanding
Trust
Success
Strength
Persistence
Patience
Passion
Love
Listening
Honesty
Gratitude
Forgiveness
Enthusiasm
Determination
Courage
Confidence
Commitment
Authenticity
Acceptance
Abundance

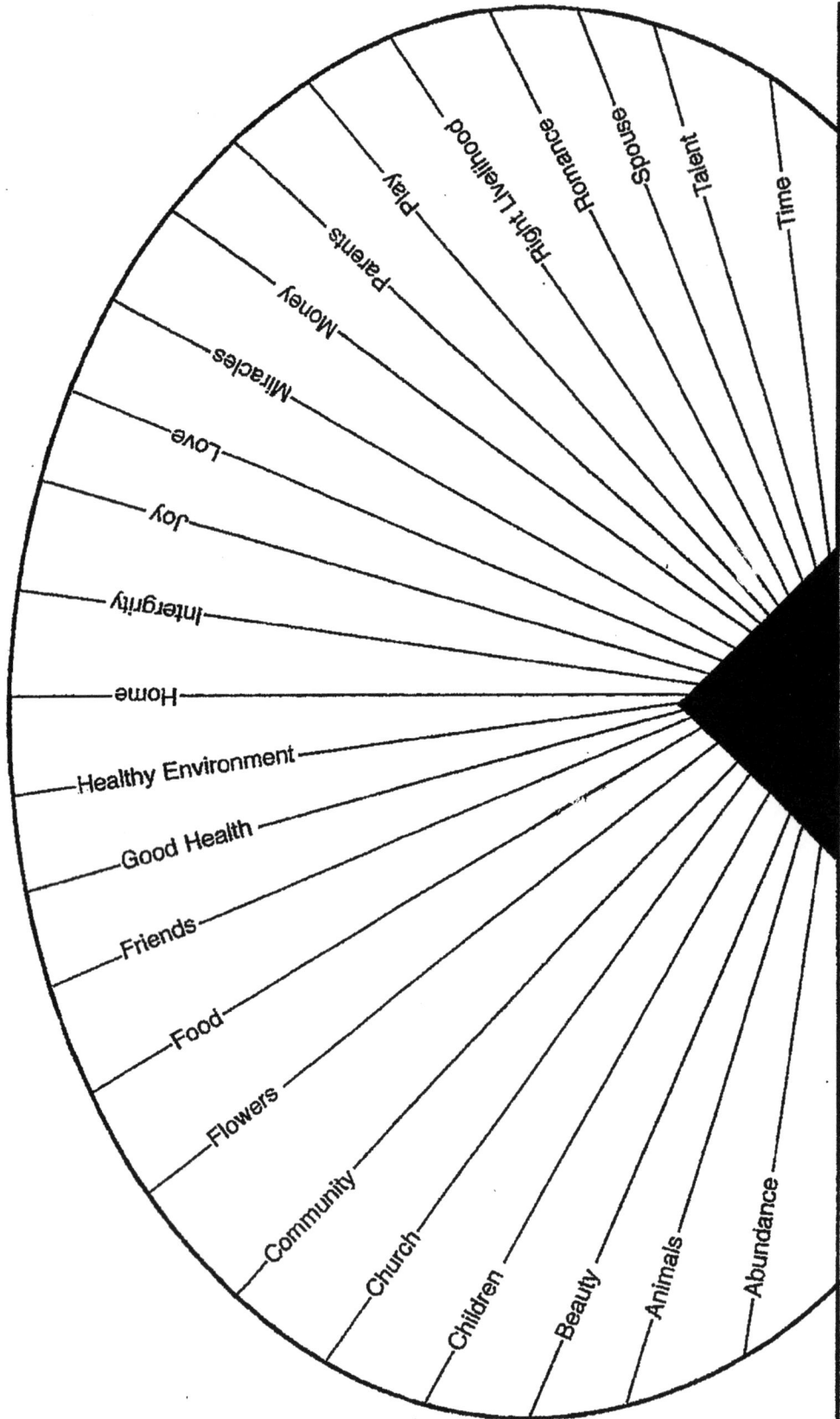

Blessings (Chart 11)

Time
Talent
Spouse
Romance
Right Livelihood
Play
Parents
Money
Miracles
Love
Joy
Intergrity
Home
Healthy Environment
Good Health
Friends
Food
Flowers
Community
Church
Children
Beauty
Animals
Abundance

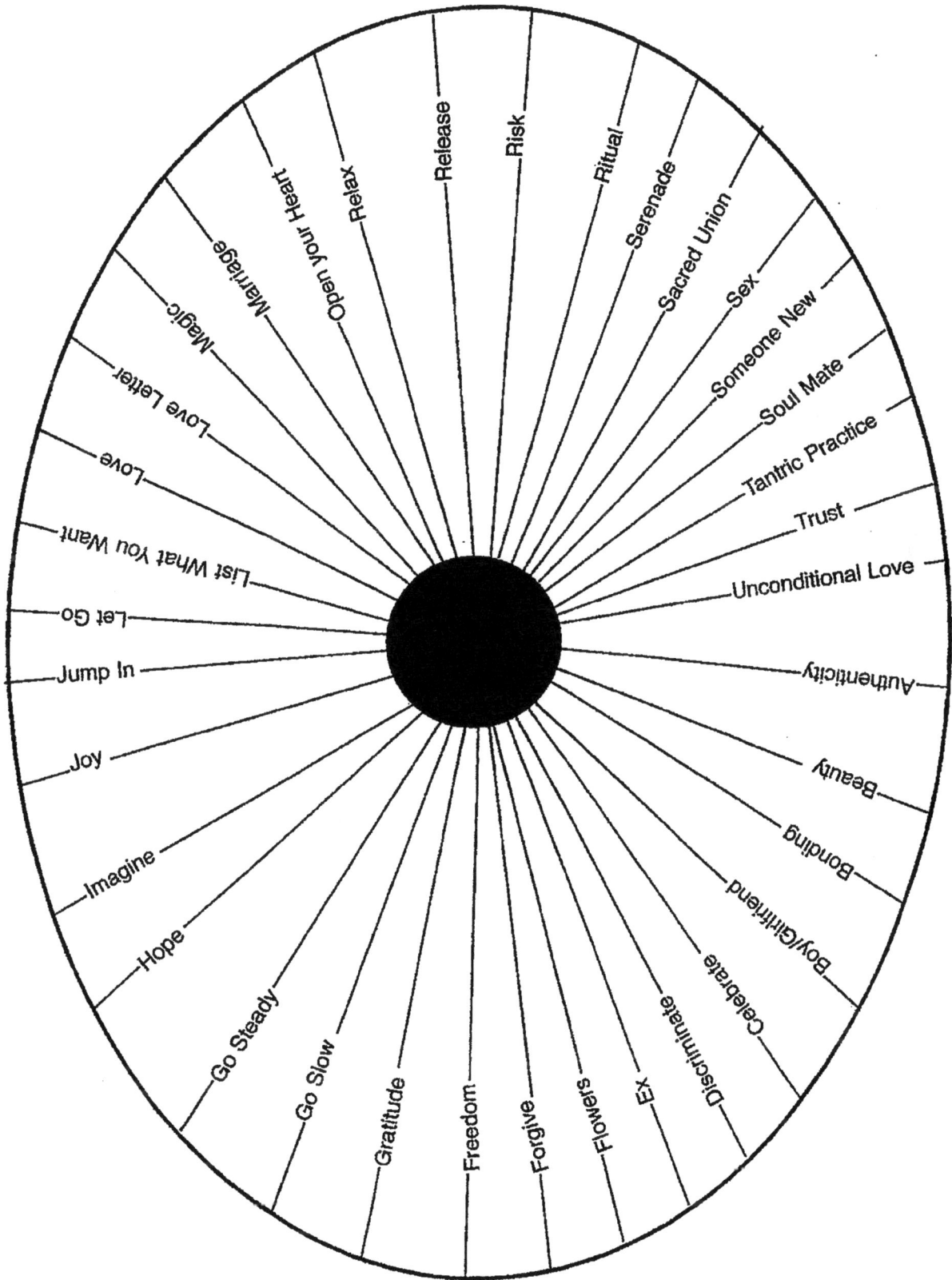

Love & Romance (Chart 12)

Release
Risk
Relax
Ritual
Open your Heart
Serenade
Marriage
Sacred Union
Magic
Sex
Love Letter
Someone New
Love
Soul Mate
List What You Want
Tantric Practice
Let Go
Trust
Jump In
Unconditional Love
Joy
Authenticity
Imagine
Beauty
Hope
Bonding
Go Steady
Boy/Girlfriend
Go Slow
Celebrate
Gratitude
Discriminate
Freedom
Ex
Forgive
Flowers

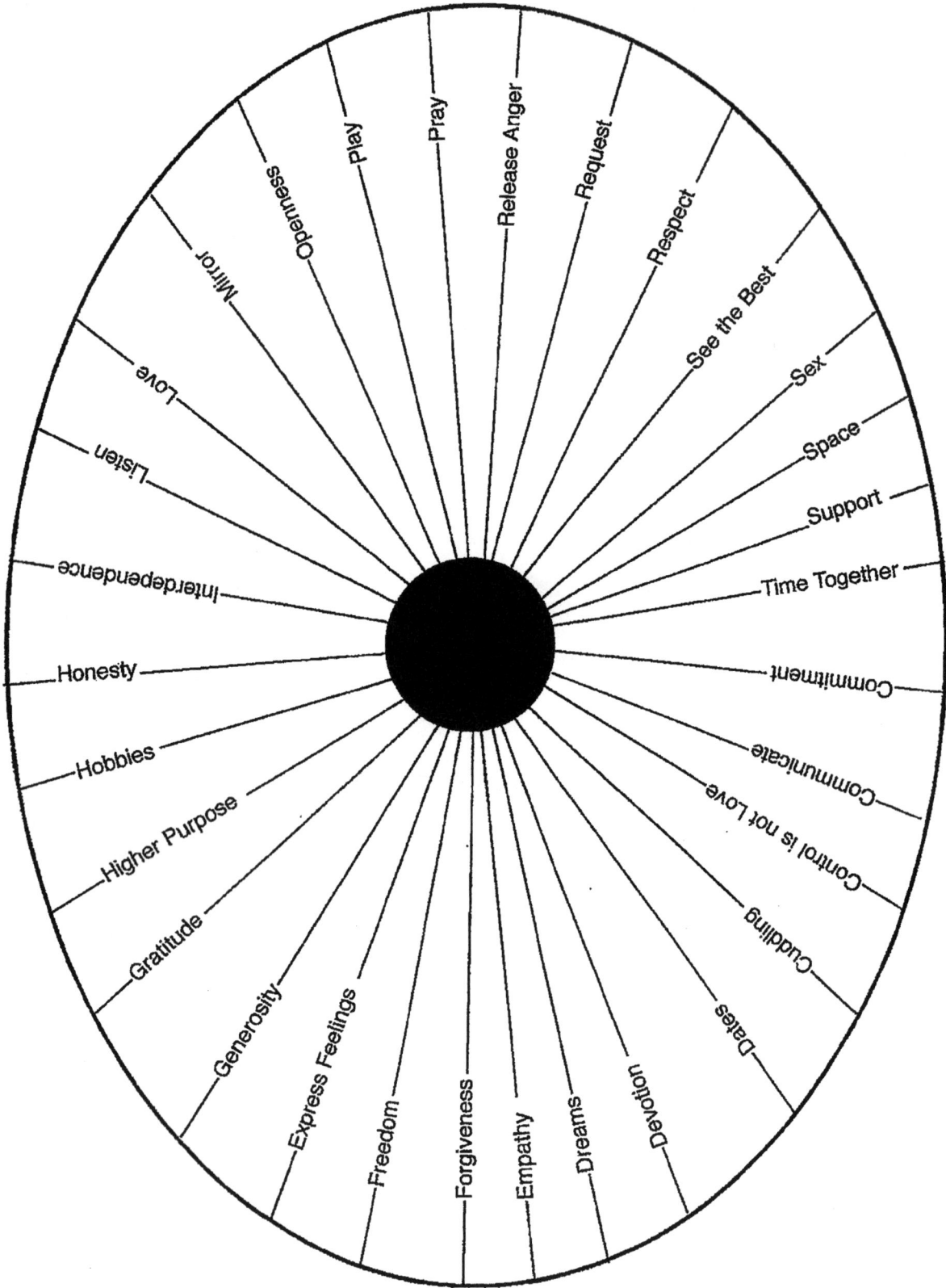

Nurturing Relationships (Chart 13)

Play
Pray
Release Anger
Request
Respect
See the Best
Sex
Space
Support
Time Together
Commitment
Communicate
Control is not Love
Cuddling
Dates
Devotion
Dreams
Empathy
Forgiveness
Freedom
Express Feelings
Generosity
Gratitude
Higher Purpose
Hobbies
Honesty
Interdependence
Listen
Love
Mirror
Openness

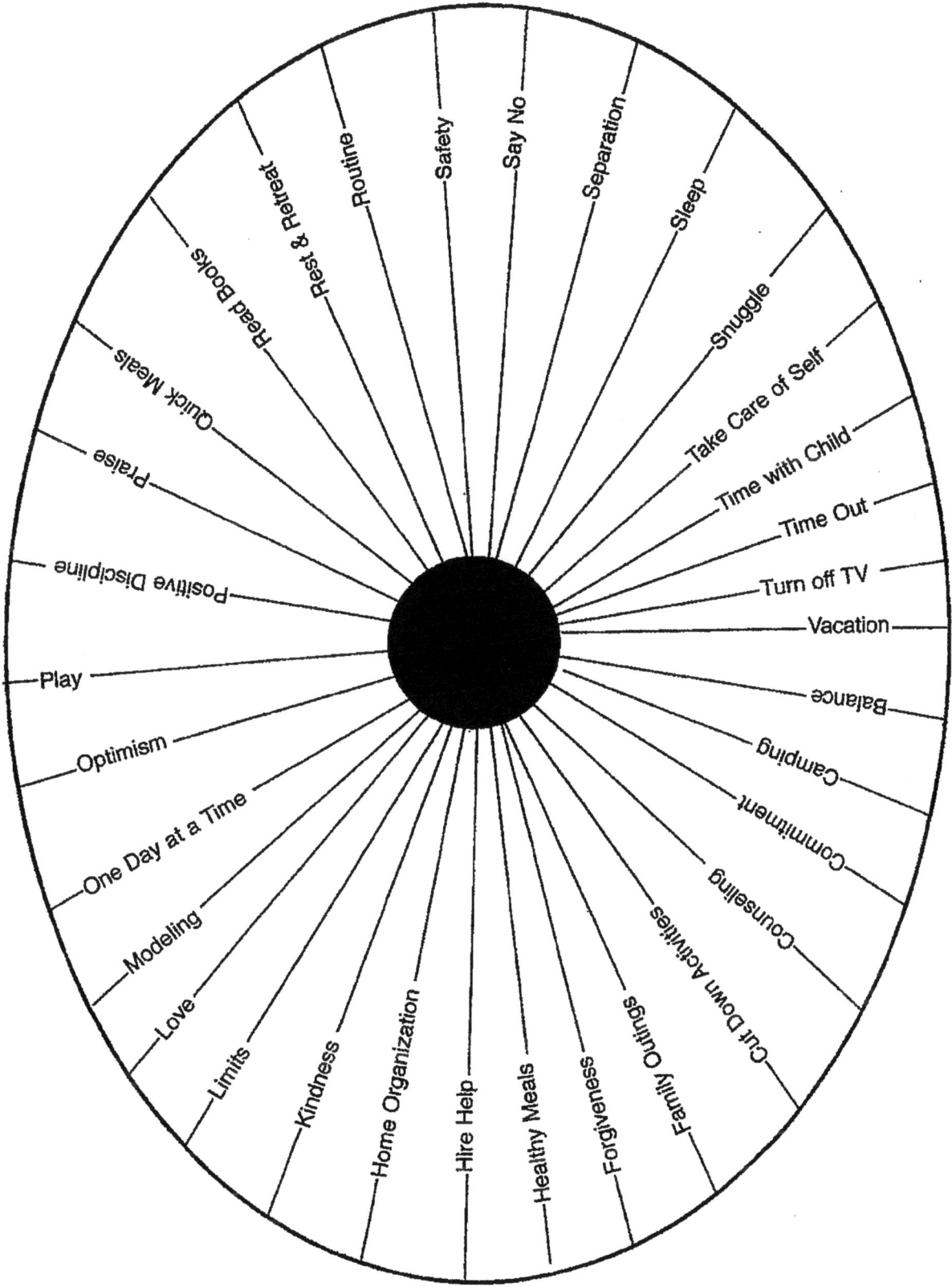

Parenting (Chart 14)

Safety
Say No
Separation
Sleep
Snuggle
Take Care of Self
Time with Child
Time Out
Turn off TV
Vacation
Balance
Camping
Commitment
Counseling
Cut Down Activities
Family Outings
Forgiveness
Healthy Meals
Hire Help
Home Organization
Kindness
Limits
Love
Modeling
One Day at a Time
Optimism
Play
Positive Discipline
Praise
Quick Meals
Read Books
Rest & Retreat
Routine

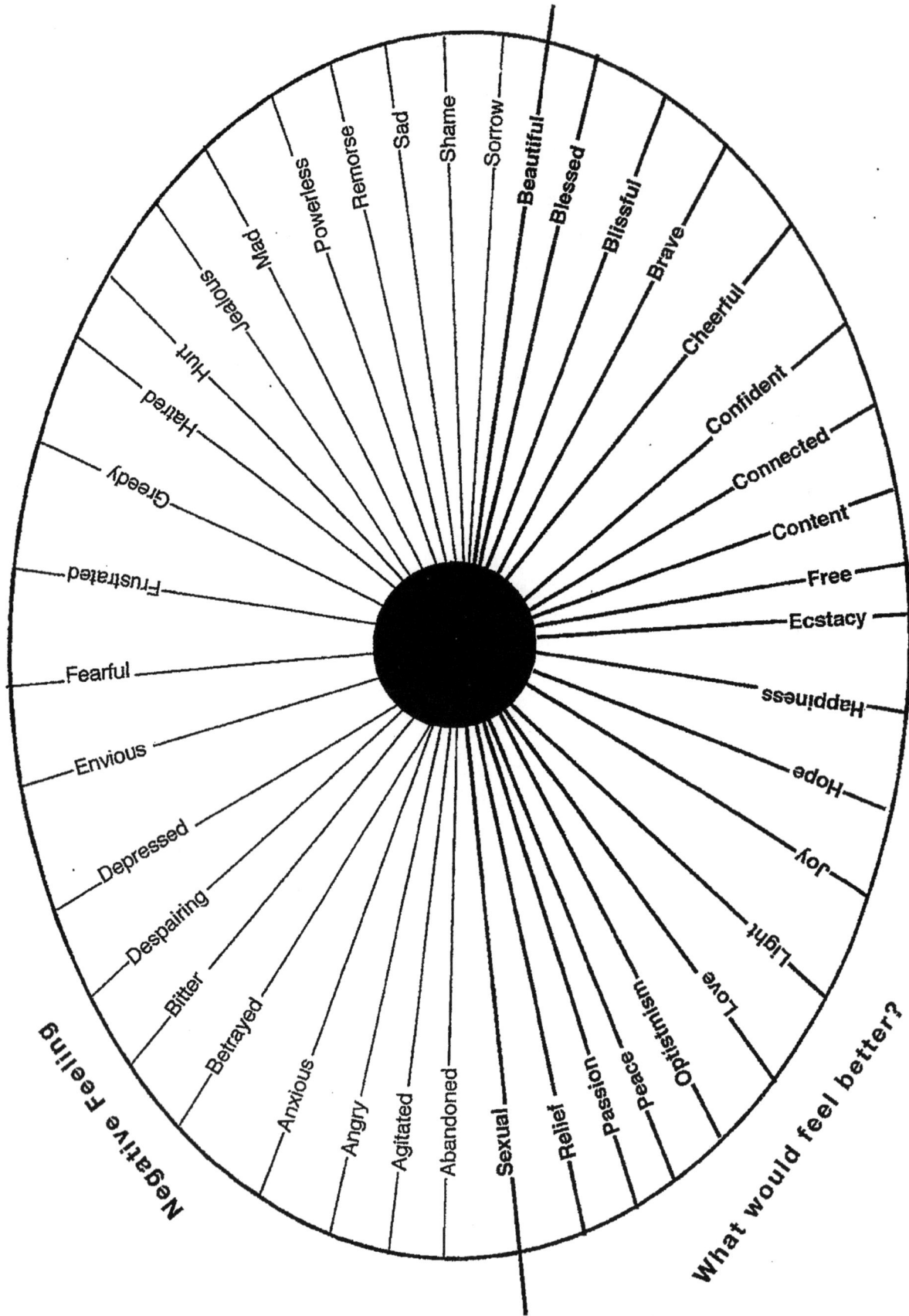

Feelings (Chart 15)

Negative Feeling

What would feel better?

Mad
Powerless
Jealous
Remorse
Hurt
Sad
Hatred
Shame
Greedy
Sorrow
Frustrated
Beautiful
Fearful
Blessed
Envious
Blissful
Depressed
Brave
Despairing
Cheerful
Bitter
Confident
Betrayed
Connected
Anxious
Content
Angry
Free
Agitated
Ecstacy
Abandoned
Happiness
Sexual
Hope
Relief
Joy
Passion
Light
Peace
Love
Optimism

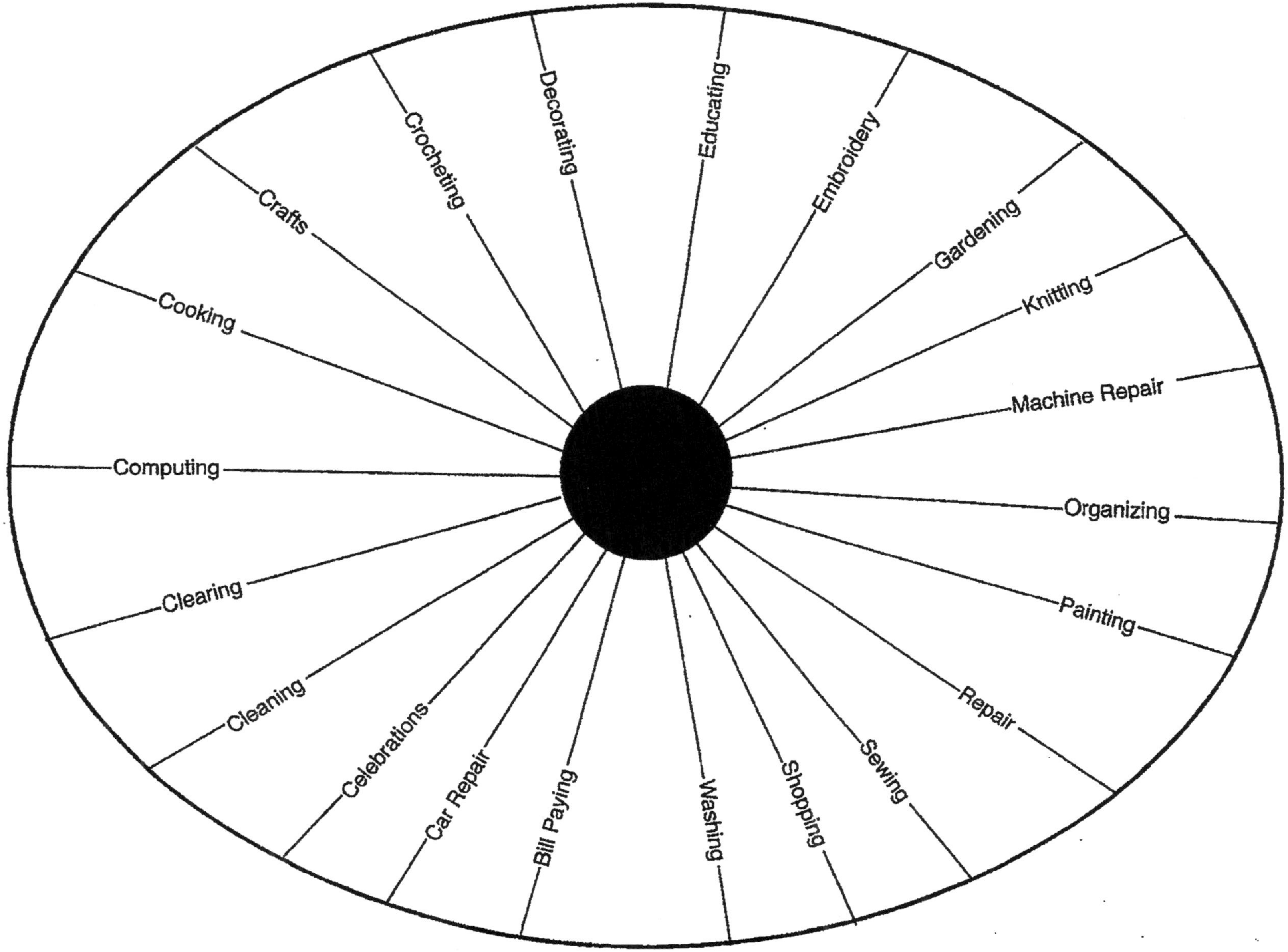
Decorating
Educating
Crocheting
Embroidery
Crafts
Gardening
Knitting
Cooking
Machine Repair
Computing
Organizing
Clearing
Painting
Cleaning
Repair
Celebrations
Car Repair
Bill Paying
Washing
Shopping
Sewing

Home Arts (Chart 16)

Home Problem Solving (Chart 17)

Obstacles

- Attention
- Clean
- Clear Energy
- Donate Stuff
- Enjoy
- Family Meeting
- Feng Shui
- Hire Help
- Love
- Move
- Music
- Organize
- Relax
- Remodel
- Repair
- Replace
- Share Chores
- Simplify
- Time at Home
- Yard Sale
- Lack of Privacy
- Location
- Noisy
- Disorganized
- High Housing Costs
- Other
- Stuck Energy
- Size
- Too Many Chores
- Too Much Stuff
- Too Little Money

Solutions

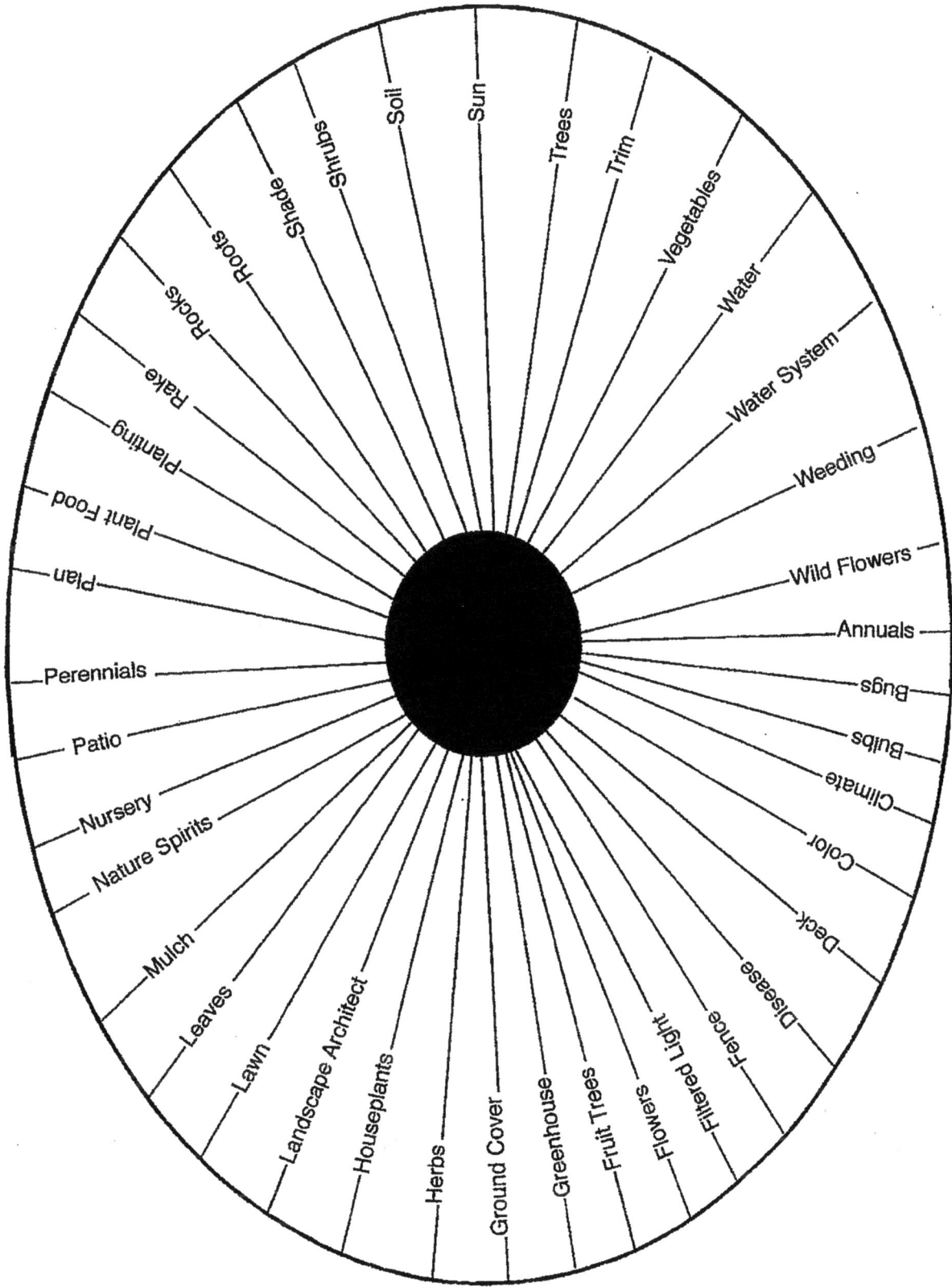

Gardening (Chart 18)

Sun, Trees, Trim, Vegetables, Water, Water System, Weeding, Wild Flowers, Annuals, Bugs, Bulbs, Climate, Color, Deck, Disease, Fence, Filtered Light, Flowers, Fruit Trees, Greenhouse, Ground Cover, Herbs, Houseplants, Landscape Architect, Lawn, Leaves, Mulch, Nature Spirits, Nursery, Patio, Perennials, Plan, Plant Food, Planting, Rake, Rocks, Roots, Shade, Shrubs, Soil

Personal Finance Problem Solving (Chart 19)

Obstacles

- Shopping Addiction
- Record Keeping
- Over Extended
- Money Addiction
- Low Income
- Job Loss
- Greed
- Fear
- Depression
- Recession
- National Economy
- Local Economy
- Cash Flow
- Bills
- Trust

Solutions

- Ask for a Raise
- Be Responsible
- Be Self Supporting
- Cut Expenses
- Cut Up Credit Cards
- Find Free Options
- Get a Second Job
- Go on a Money Diet
- Hire a Financial Planner
- Invest in Mutual Funds
- Invest in Property
- Invest in Stocks
- Pay Off Credit Card
- Reduce Rent
- Save
- Shop in Bulk
- Stop present Giving
- Take an Investment Class
- Take a Money Class
- Take a Prosperity Class
- Tithe Money, Time or Talent

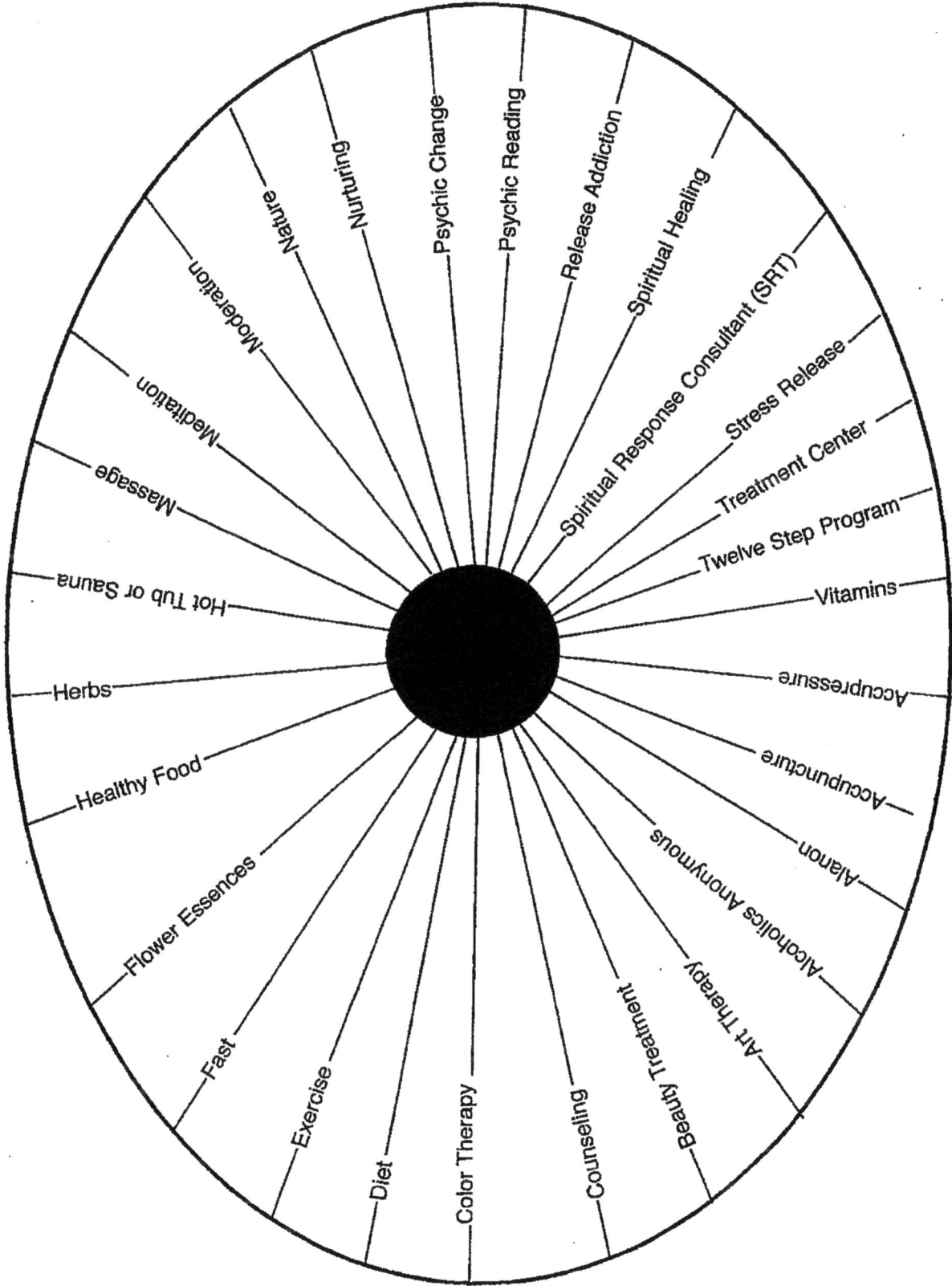

Healing Arts (Chart 20)

Nature
Nurturing
Psychic Change
Psychic Reading
Release Addiction
Spiritual Healing
Spiritual Response Consultant (SRT)
Stress Release
Treatment Center
Twelve Step Program
Vitamins
Acupressure
Acupuncture
Al-anon
Alcoholics Anonymous
Art Therapy
Beauty Treatment
Counseling
Color Therapy
Diet
Exercise
Fast
Flower Essences
Healthy Food
Herbs
Hot Tub or Sauna
Massage
Meditation
Moderation

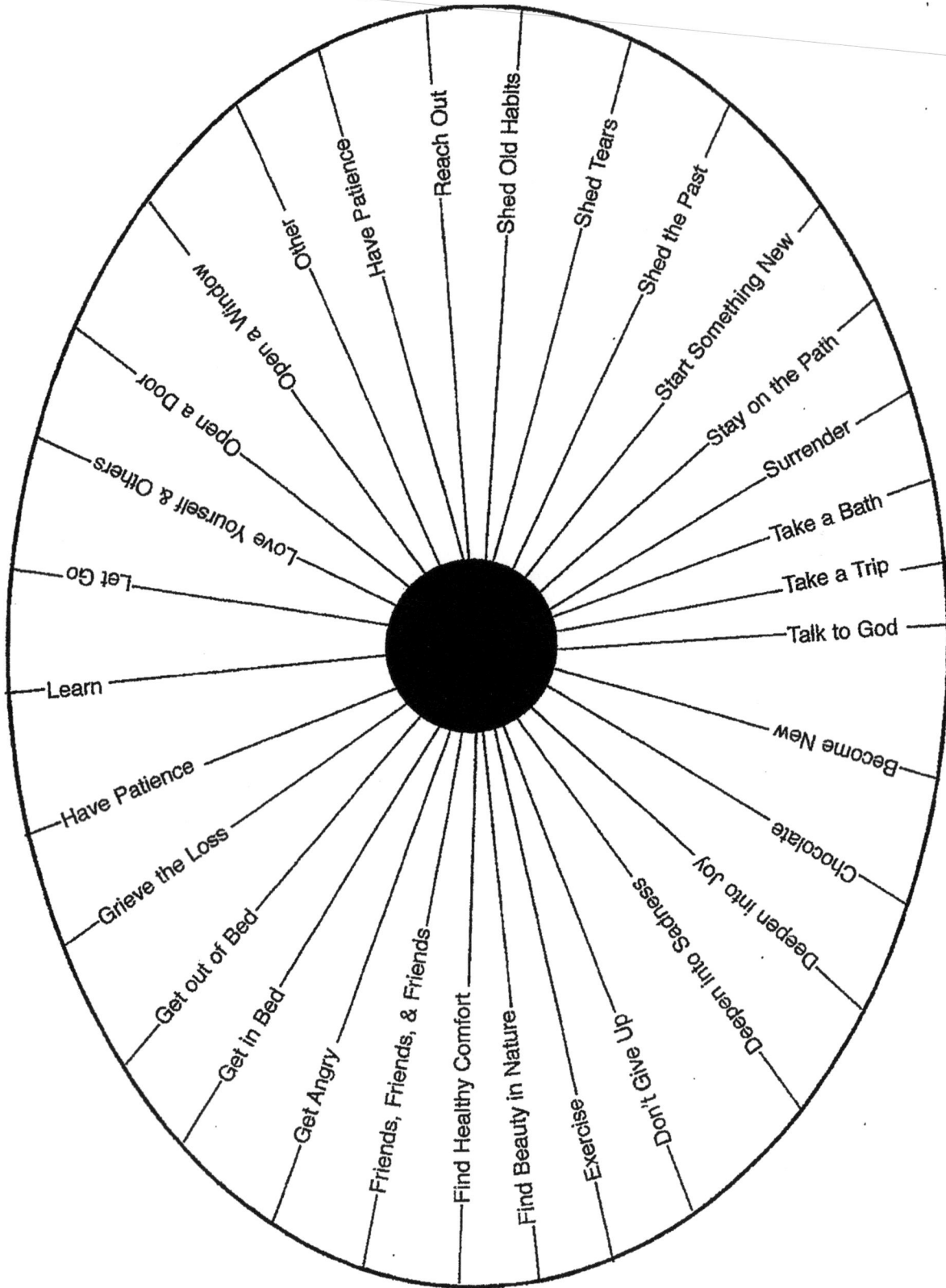

Life Transitions (Chart 21)

Reach Out
Have Patience
Other
Open a Window
Open a Door
Love Yourself & Others
Let Go
Learn
Have Patience
Grieve the Loss
Get out of Bed
Get in Bed
Get Angry
Friends, Friends, & Friends
Find Healthy Comfort
Find Beauty in Nature
Exercise
Don't Give Up
Deepen into Sadness
Deepen into Joy
Chocolate
Become New
Talk to God
Take a Trip
Take a Bath
Surrender
Stay on the Path
Start Something New
Shed the Past
Shed Tears
Shed Old Habits

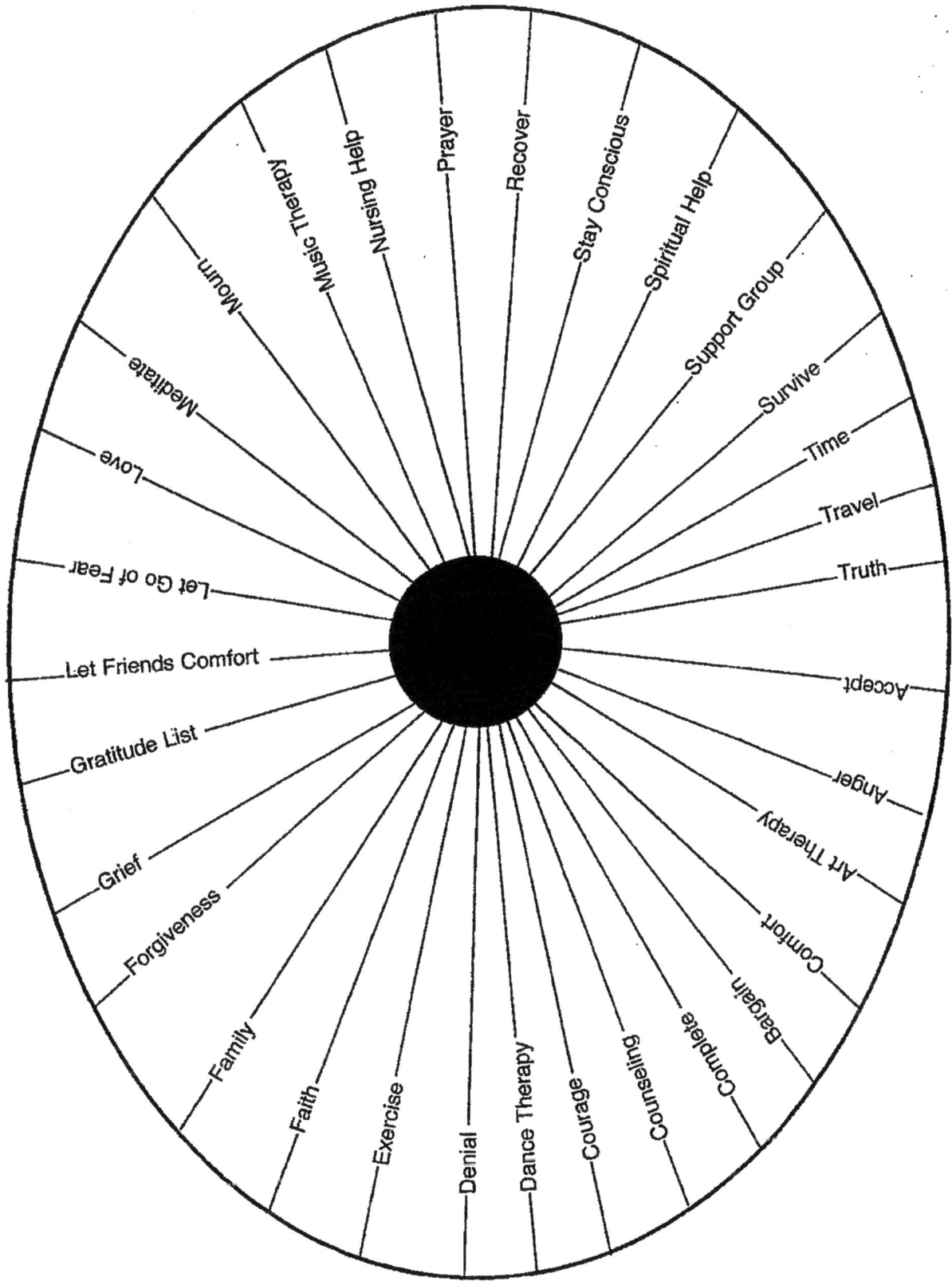

Death & Letting Go (Chart 22)

Prayer
Recover
Stay Conscious
Spiritual Help
Support Group
Survive
Time
Travel
Truth
Accept
Anger
Art Therapy
Comfort
Bargain
Complete
Counseling
Courage
Dance Therapy
Denial
Exercise
Faith
Family
Forgiveness
Grief
Gratitude List
Let Friends Comfort
Let Go of Fear
Love
Meditate
Mourn
Music Therapy
Nursing Help

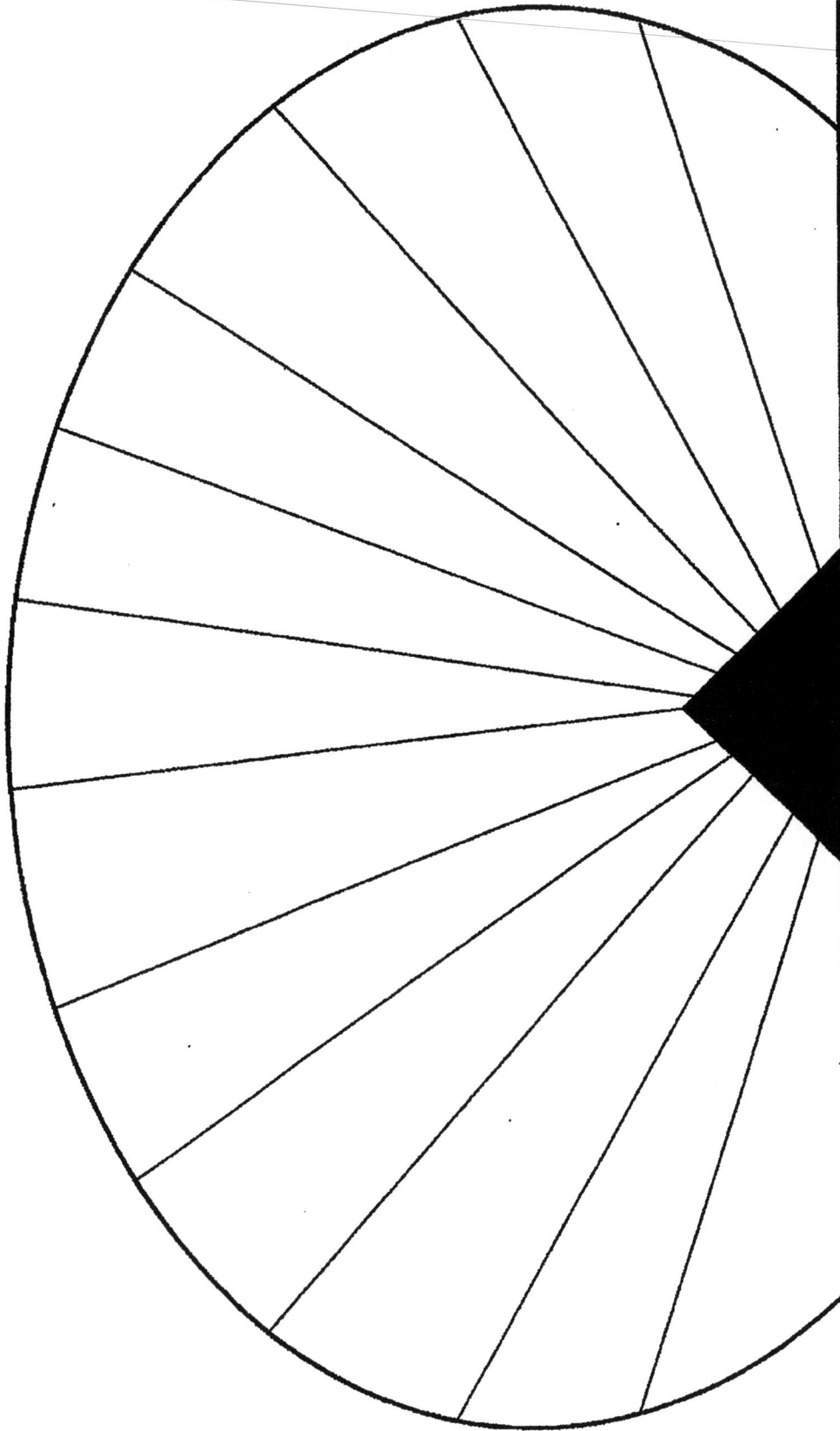

Your Own Chart (Chart 23)

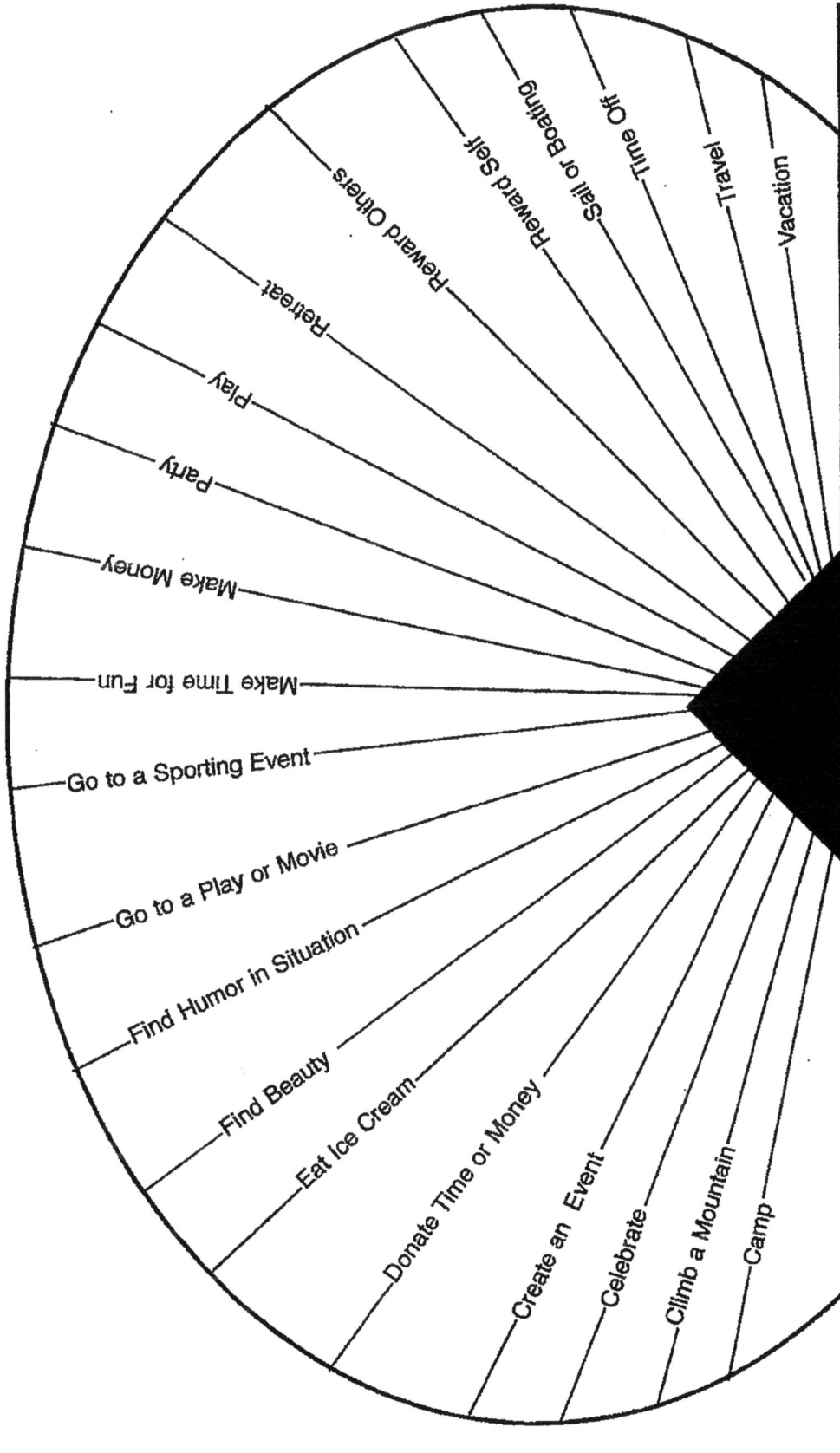

Fun & Adventure (Chart 24)

- Vacation
- Travel
- Time Off
- Sail or Boating
- Reward Self
- Reward Others
- Retreat
- Play
- Party
- Make Money
- Make Time for Fun
- Go to a Sporting Event
- Go to a Play or Movie
- Find Humor in Situation
- Find Beauty
- Eat Ice Cream
- Donate Time or Money
- Create an Event
- Celebrate
- Climb a Mountain
- Camp

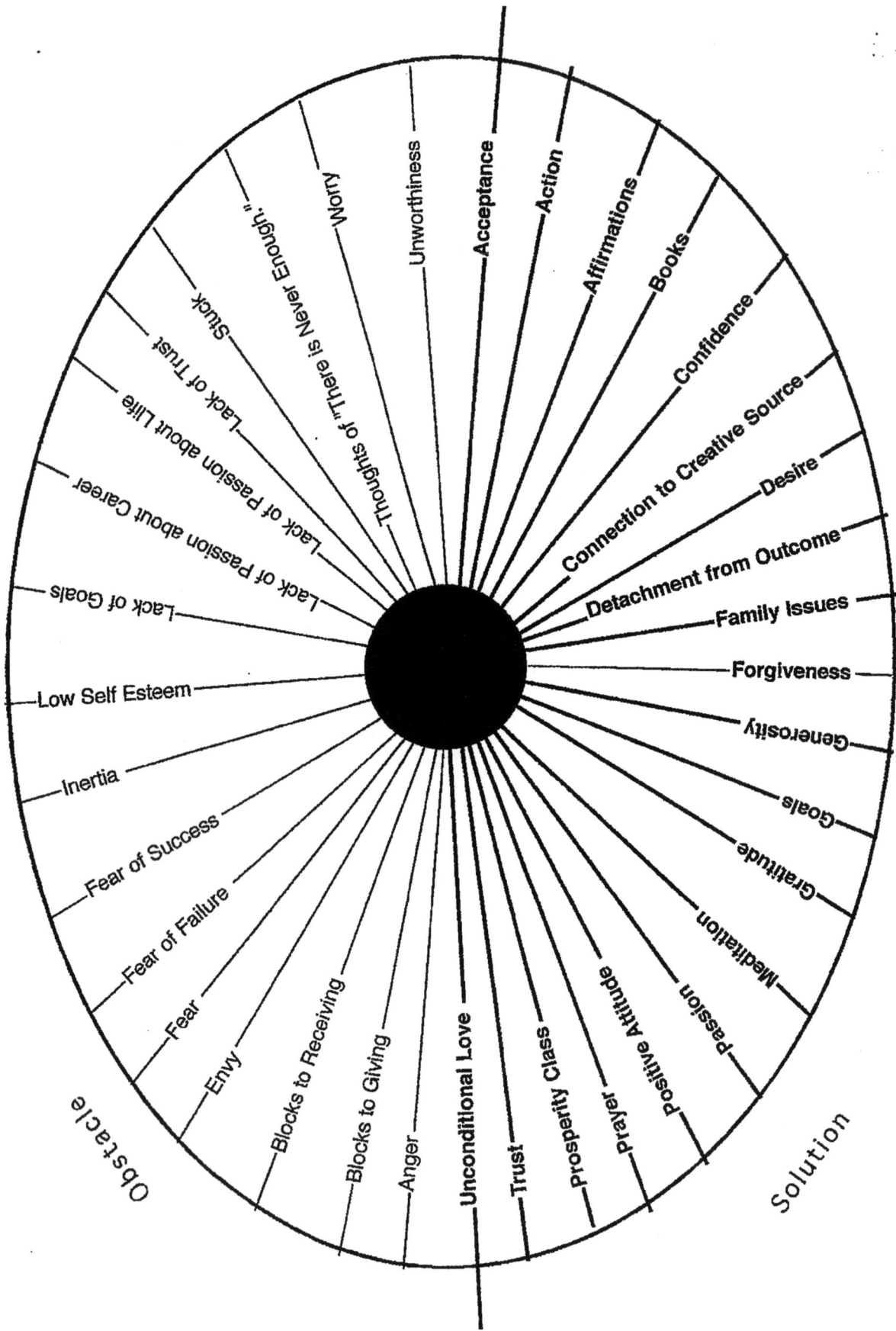

Prosperity Problem Solving (Chart 25)

Obstacle

- Unworthiness
- Worry
- Thoughts of "There is Never Enough."
- Stuck
- Lack of Trust
- Lack of Passion about Life
- Lack of Passion about Career
- Lack of Goals
- Low Self Esteem
- Inertia
- Fear of Success
- Fear of Failure
- Fear
- Envy
- Blocks to Receiving
- Blocks to Giving
- Anger

Solution

- Acceptance
- Action
- Affirmations
- Books
- Confidence
- Connection to Creative Source
- Desire
- Detachment from Outcome
- Family Issues
- Forgiveness
- Generosity
- Goals
- Gratitude
- Meditation
- Passion
- Positive Attitude
- Prayer
- Prosperity Class
- Trust
- Unconditional Love

About Joan Rose Staffen

Joan Rose is a writer, artist and intuitive consultant. She is the author of *Divination & Joy, Divination & Action, Divination and Art Charts,* and *Catching You, Catching Me, Catching Fire.* Joan is dedicated to assisting others to heal their lives, rediscover their purpose, and stay on their life path. She helps her clients uncover, visualize, plan, and actualize their dreams through her books and experiential workshops teaching divination, spirituality, creativity and prosperity methods.

Visit her websites at writestarpublishing.com or joanroseart.com for further information. She can be reached at joan@jointsolutions.com for consultations.

Made in the USA
San Bernardino, CA
29 April 2017